A
WESTERN
FRONT
COMPANION
1914–1918

A–Z SOURCE TO THE BATTLES, WEAPONS,
PEOPLE, PLACES, AIR COMBAT

T0204580

By the same author

A
WESTERN
FRONT
COMPANION
1914–1918

A–Z SOURCE TO THE BATTLES, WEAPONS,
PEOPLE, PLACES, AIR COMBAT

JOHN LAFFIN

SUTTON PUBLISHING LIMITED

First published in the United Kingdom in 1994
Alan Sutton Publishing Limited, an imprint of Sutton Publishing Limited
Phoenix Mill · Thrupp · Stroud · Gloucestershire

Paperback edition first published 1997

British Library Cataloguing-in-Publication Data

Laffin, John
    Western Front Companion, 1914–18 : A–Z
    Source to the Battles, Weapons, People,
    Places, Air Combat
    1. Title
    940.4144

ISBN 0-7509-1520-X

Library of Congress Cataloging-in-Publication Data applied for

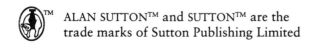 ™ ALAN SUTTON™ and SUTTON™ are the
trade marks of Sutton Publishing Limited

Typeset in 11/15 Sabon.
Typesetting and origination by
Sutton Publishing Limited.
Printed and bound in Great Britain by
Butler & Tanner Ltd, Frome, Somerset.

CONTENTS

AUTHOR'S NOTE & ACKNOWLEDGEMENTS

A Western Front Companion is the result of decades of experience and study of the Western Front. In that period my wife Hazelle – my personal Western Front companion – and I have spent an aggregate of more than five years on the battlefields of France and Flanders, long enough to warrant a long-service medal, if such an award existed for the Western Front.

The need for such a book has been apparent to me for many years. Hundreds, probably thousands, of pilgrims and tourists meeting me on the battlefields have asked questions about the conflict on the Western Front. What *is* the Western Front? What were the major battles? What weapons did the soldiers use? Why were there such catastrophic losses? And much else. This book answers many questions and anticipates others, though it is not a guidebook in the conventional sense since such books are already available.

A Western Front Companion is much more than a guidebook, for it provides a basic understanding of the phenomenon which we call the Western Front, in all its military and human complexity. The Western Front was a way of death and a way of life for millions of men and it left a scar across the soul of their respective nations.

Over the years various people have been helpful to me and to Hazelle in the writing of this book and many others about the Western Front. Those who deserve our particular thanks include Anny De Decker, Tony De Bruyne, Jean-Pierre Thierry, Martial Delebarre, Jean Letaille, Yves Föhlen and Marcel Robidoux. Members and former members of the Commonwealth War Graves Commission have also assisted us, notably Steve Grady, Jacky White, Norman Christie, Colette Vanderville and Jouelle Scalbert.

Throughout my life as a military historian innumerable British, Australian, Canadian, New Zealand, French and German veterans of the First World War have shared their wartime experiences with me. Alas, few of them survive but the book serves as a form of memorial for them.

The illustrations in this book, photographs, paintings and sketches, are from my own collection unless otherwise indicated.

CHAPTER ONE

CREATING THE WESTERN FRONT

The Western Front is probably the best-known battle line in history, but the events which led to its creation need explanation and clarification. Without this help what are people of the late twentieth century to make of this extraordinary area and the astonishing events that took place there? In simple terms, the Western Front was a relatively narrow battlefield 460 miles in length and up to 20 miles in breadth on which, during a period of 50 months, more than 6 million soldiers were killed and another 14 million wounded.

To expand the description a little, vast armies confronted one another across belts of barbed wire many miles deep. The wire defended line after line of trenches that collectively ran for thousands of miles across a morass of mud, and in places hills and mountains. The hostility between the Allies and the Central Powers was intense and their soldiers fought ferociously, but for most of the time with little military result.

A mixture of political and military madness brought the Western Front into being and maintained the incredible violence, which made it so infamous. The nature of the war, the prodigious effort, limitless courage and sacrifice – on both sides – and the intensity of the fighting has intrigued those generations that followed the 'lost generation'. There is a curious fascination with the Western Front and all that it entails – the memorials and monuments, the mine craters and trenches, the famous woods and rivers, the thousands of war cemeteries, the villages and towns with names that would excite not a moment's attention had they not been the scene of some costly battle. Like the battlefields of Waterloo and Gallipoli and those of the English Civil War and the American Civil War, the killing fields of the Western Front have an apparently inextinguishable mystique.

The Western Front differs from the others in that fighting raged across it almost incessantly for the duration of the war. The death of 20,000 men in one day of battle was not cataclysmic enough to bring the madness to an end. Neither side could break through the other's lines, no matter the force, the money and the lives expended.

The trigger for what came to be called 'The Great War' was a singular act of madness. It was the assassination, on

28 June 1914, of the Archduke Franz Ferdinand, the heir to the Austro-Hungarian Empire, and of his wife. The murders took place in the Bosnian city of Sarajevo and the killer was a young student nationalist, Gavrilo Princip. The organization to which Princip belonged, Mlada Bosnia (Young Bosnia), considered his act 'tyrannicide for the common good'.

Franz Ferdinand was undoubtedly a tyrant, as well as being a brutal, boastful and bloody-minded man. As a pitiless hunter he shot tens of thousands of birds and animals and fired his guns and rifles so frequently that he permanently injured his shoulder and impaired his hearing.

As a prince Franz Ferdinand was also a field marshal and he had gone to Bosnia and its sister province Hercegovina, which the Habsburgs had annexed in 1908, to inspect the Austrian Army. The populace of the province, a mixture of Slavs, Serbs and Croats, had always wanted to join Serbia, their national state, and they regarded the Austrians as a hostile occupying power. In killing the Habsburg royal couple Gavrilo Princip imagined that he was striking a blow for freedom.

Austria-Hungary saw the assassination as a challenge to its status as a Great Power, especially as its rulers had already had other trouble with Serbia. The Habsburgs asked their German allies to back them in a show of force and the German Emperor Wilhelm II and his chancellor, Bethmann Hollweg, not only promised support but said that if Russia intervened to aid Serbia Germany would oppose Russia.

Uncertain about how to proceed, the government in Vienna took until 23 July to frame a formal note to be sent to Serbia. Its 'Ten Points' included cessation of all propaganda against Austria-Hungary, the arrest of certain people accused of complicity in the assassination, and the participation of Austrian representatives during the investigations in Serbia. The general intention was to humiliate Serbia.

However, the Serbians accepted the note, though they added qualifications to a few points in an attempt to salvage a little prestige. As a precaution, the armed forces were mobilized. On the whole, the Serbian official reply, handed to the Austrian minister in Belgrade, was such a cleverly drawn document that Vienna did not know how to react. It solved the problem, on 28 July, by declaring war on Serbia, though the Austro-Hungarian army was in no state to do any actual fighting.

Russia, as patron of the Slav states in the Balkans, felt itself threatened and began to mobilize its huge army of conscripts. Even now nothing more than grandiose bluffing was in progress, but German military might and pride became involved. General Schleiffen, chief of the German general staff from 1892 to 1906, had enunciated the dictum 'Mobilization means war', and although he was dead his slogan lived on.

The German general staff convinced themselves that a war was actually in progress and on this false premise argued that if they did not act now they would lose their great advantage of superior speed and sophisticated railway transport. Their paranoid fear was that Russia and France, as allies, would attack them on two fronts, – an alarming prospect. On 31 July Chancellor Bethmann Hollwegg asked his chief of the general staff, von Moltke, just one question: 'Is the Fatherland in danger?'

'Yes,' said Moltke, a response that led directly to war. Even so, some statesmen were still trying to mediate in an effort to prevent war. In the early hours of 1 August, King George V appealed directly to Tsar Nicholas of Russia to refrain from hostilities. But the momentum towards war was now unstoppable and on that same evening Russia and Germany were at war. On 3 August Germany declared war against France.

On 2 August the Germans had demanded that Belgium give the German armies open thoroughfare across the little lowland country in order to attack France. The German general staff wanted to implement the Schleiffen Plan, or the Cannae Plan as Schleiffen himself called it. It was an imaginative and ambitious strategy to encircle the French armies in the event of another war. Though he was now dead, Schleiffen's plan was still attractive to his successors.

When King Albert of Belgium refused to comply with the Germans' wishes the British government was drawn into the conflict because of a treaty, dating back to 1839, which committed Britain to go to Belgium's defence should it be attacked. On 4 August Britain became the only power to declare war on Germany, rather than the other way round.

The chain of reactions was moving so quickly that nobody could stop one declaration linking with another and suddenly the world was at war. Both sides were convinced that their cause was right and that God marched with them; German soldiers' belt buckles carried the words *Got mit uns* (God with us).

Immense armies were soon on the march to the eastern and western fronts – that is, the *German* eastern and western fronts. In the east the more professional and better-armed Germans decisively defeated the Russian armies at Tannenberg at the end of August. Vast German and French armies could move rapidly towards the Western Front because of the efficient railway systems but once they were delivered to the railheads the troops' movement was slow, since no army had any mechanical transport. The initial thrust provided military momentum for only a month, after which the armies moved no faster than in Napoleon's time, a century earlier.

Defence was largely mechanized, because of the railways, but attack was not. Horses pulled the guns and the transport while forage for the horses occupied more space than ammunition or food.

On 14 August the French launched a great offensive at Lorraine and suffered casualties so heavy that they were not exceeded in any later campaign, including that of Verdun. The Germans swept through Belgium, with the soldiers sometimes covering 30 miles a day on foot. Each time the French generals ordered a major attack against the invaders they lost still more men.

The British, meanwhile, were deciding how best to help Belgium, and at a Council of War on 5 August several ideas were presented. After long discussion, much of it

A French drawing of August 1914 showing the French Army going to the rescue of the damsel Alsace. The German claim to sovereignty over Alsace is swept aside as the French troops arrive.

pointless, Sir Henry Wilson of the War Office pointed out that the British Expeditionary Force, although it was a small one of about 100,000, must move to a timetable drawn up in 1911 and the only one in existence. It placed the BEF on the French left. This couldn't possibly help Belgium, the reason for Britain going to war, but the Council of War agreed to use the old plan, the cabinet concurred and the BEF was sent to the Western Front. We can only speculate on what might have been achieved had the BEF been kept as an independent force and used more intelligently.

By 22 August advance divisions of the BEF had reached the town of Mons, where the following day they were attacked by two German army corps, vastly superior in numbers. The BEF held firm but as the French troops on the right fell back the British commander, General Sir John French, had no option but to retreat. At Le Cateau on 26 August the BEF stood and fought again and withdrew once more.

In fact, both sides were moving away from each other, but the French and Germans again collided after 5 September when the Germans crossed the Marne. In an impossibly confused situation, because of nonexistent or inadequate communications, remarkable events occurred. For instance, the BEF advanced to find no opposition whatever, but instead of pushing on vigorously the generals advanced at only 8 miles a day. Nevertheless, under the French onslaught

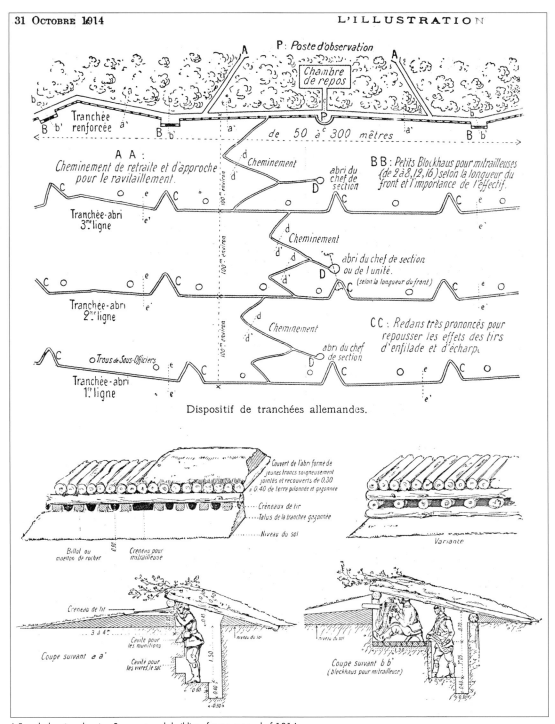

A French drawing showing German trench building, from a manual of 1914.

the German armies fell back and senior Allied officers spoke confidently of being in Germay within a month. The Allied pursuit lasted a mere five days. On 14 September the exhausted Germans crossed the Aisne and here set up a desperate and inadequate defence.

They were astounded when the advancing Allies stopped. This gave the Germans time to entrench, and this they promptly did, setting up machine guns to protect their lines. Trench warfare had begun. Since the lines of both sides 'hung in the air' – that is, they had no defended ends – there was still a chance for one side to turn the other's flank.

General Joffre, the French commander, was too dull to see the value of aiding the Belgian Army besieged in Antwerp. In any case, he disliked the Belgians, reason enough in his case to deny them any assistance. The British Secretary of State for War, Lord Kitchener, also failed to grasp the importance of Antwerp. The one man who did see the port's strategic importance was Winston Churchill, then First Lord of the Admiralty. He rushed 3,000 Royal Marines to Antwerp but they

14

The first can be obviated by hanging a sack from the top of the plate which goes over the sniper's head, like the black cloth of a photographer.

The second one can be obviated by placing the steel plate far forward towards the outer crest of the parapet and thus reduce the depth and size of the embrasure. If this is not possible, it is as well to make dummy embrasures exactly similar to the real one all along the parapet.

III.—TRENCHES.

SAND-BAG REVETMENT.

1. A great many of the sand-bag revetments are giving way or "bulging." This is entirely owing to the faulty manner in which they have originally been built.

The common faults are :—

(a) The revetments are built perpendicularly instead of at a slope of one in four.

(b) Joints are not broken, i.e., joints in contiguous rows of sand-bags coincide.

(c) The bottom row is a "stretcher."

(d) The top row is also a "stretcher."

2. Sand-bag revetments must be built as follows :—

(a) Commence with a row of "headers," the front portion of the header on ground level, the back sloped back to give a slope of one in four, i.e., if sand-bag is 24 inch long, the back should be sunk 6 inch.

(b) Second row all "stretchers" or alternative "headers" and "stretchers," taking care to break joint with first row.

(c) Third row all "headers," breaking joint with second row.

(d) And so on, odd rows all "headers," even rows all "stretchers" or alternate "headers" and "stretchers."

(e) Top row must be "headers."

3. To make the revetment still more secure, long sharp-pointed stakes should be driven through the sand-bags in the "headers" rows at intervals.

4. As the building progresses the earth should be heaped up at the back, level with the last row that has been laid.

5. The sand-bags should be only two-thirds filled with earth and, as they are laid, should be well beaten with the flat of a spade so as to get them square and as much like bricks as possible.

6. The "chokes" (i.e., the openings) of the "headers" should always be inwards, so that if they come undone the earth will not dribble into the trench.

15

SKETCH 2.

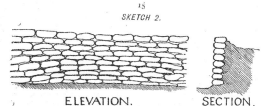

ELEVATION.   SECTION.

I. SANDBAG REVETMENT SHEWING COMMON FAULTS. viz :—

PLUMB FACE . ALL BAGS LAID AS STRETCHERS . JOINTS NOT PROPERLY BROKEN . HORIZONTAL COURSING NOT MAINTAINED . BAGS UNEVENLY FILLED . DANGEROUS STRETCHER BAG ON TOP . INADEQUATE SOIL BACKING TO PARAPET . BOTTOM COURSE ABOVE TRENCH FLOOR . BAGS NOT SPADED SQUARE .

ELEVATION   SECTION.

II. SANBAG REVETMENT SHEWING RIGHT METHOD . NOTE :—

"4 IN.I" BATTER BACK OF FACE . HEADER COURSE TOP AND BOTTOM . SUNK FOUNDATION WITH BOTTOM PERPENDICULAR TO FACE . EVENLY FILLED BAGS WELL SQUARED AND LAID BY SPADE SLAPS BONDING WITH HEADER BAGS ALTERNATELY WITH STRETCHERS HAVING JOINTS REGULARLY BROKEN AS IN BRICKWORK . THE TOP SHOULD BE GIVEN AN IRREGULAR LINE BY THROWING A FEW OLD SANDBAGS ON TOP AT INTERVALS . THESE ARE MERELY TO BREAK UP THE OUTLINE AND ARE NOT TO BE REGUARDED AS IN ANY WAY STRENGTHENING THE PARAPET .

Instructions on how to build and how not to build a trench, from a training manual of 1916.

were too small a force to be effective and on 10 October Antwerp fell. The marines were interned in nearby Holland. Escaping from Antwerp, the Belgian Army opened the sluicegates in the dykes, flooding much of the coastal areas and forcing the Germans inland.

In mid-October, the Germans and the British arrived, practically simultaneously, at Ypres, Flanders, with the intention of outflanking each other, and collided in what was later called the First Battle of Ypres. The Germans were stronger and drove a hole right through the British lines, only to be checked by courageous 'odds and sods' – cooks, batmen and unfit

soldiers. Reserves were rushed up by rail, thrown into battle and slaughtered in droves but enough men survived to hold the lines. By the end of the battle the BEF had virtually ceased to exist.

As bloody First Ypres ground to a halt, the Western Front became a fixed reality rather than a loose concept. It stretched about 460 miles from the Belgian coast at Dixmuide to a point near the French city of Belfort on the Swiss border. Everybody soon accepted the term 'Western Front', though British troops actually had to move eastwards to fight on it.

Behind the front, to the east, the Germans had captured most of France's

British troops force German soldiers from a village in 1914.

French troops capture a German standard in a Western Front action in 1915. (From a painting by François Flameng)

coal mines, all of its iron supplies and much of its heavy industry. The Germans were stronger than the Allies in the number of heavy guns and machine guns. Most importantly, they held the high ground almost everywhere. This gave them enormous strategic and tactical advantages.

Commanders on both sides spoke boldly of the great successes they would achieve in the spring of 1915. It was clear now that the war would not be over by Christmas, as British wishful thinkers had forecast. Nobody had prepared for a war of attrition and the generals did not know how to fight such a war. However, the German and French high commands were sure of one thing – millions of men would be needed to do the fighting. The Germans had an advantage here because their national birth rate had increased up to the beginning of the twentieth century. The French birth rate, on the contrary, had been declining.

In Britain Kitchener announced, to everybody's surprise, that the war would last three or four years and that Great Britain would need to raise an army of 'many millions'. He made this statement at the first cabinet meeting he attended

A hand-to-hand struggle to the death in the trenches in late 1915. The artist's impression reflected reality. (From a painting by Lucien Jonas)

and quite without reference to the Imperial General Staff, most members of which had accompanied the BEF to France. As the cabinet opposed conscription, Kitchener might have been expected to turn to the eleven divisions of the Territorial Army, but he had an unjustifiably low opinion of the part-time soldiers and instead sought volunteers.

He hoped to draw in 100,000 men in the first six months and perhaps 500,000 in all. In fact, a wave of patriotic enthusiasm brought in 500,000 volunteers in the first month and for the next eighteen months 100,000 a month joined the colours.

The army was not prepared to receive so many men but they were soon needed in the killing fields of the Western Front.

CHAPTER TWO

THE COMMANDERS

The war on the Western Front made many generals famous, or infamous, according to the view taken of the campaigns, offensives and battles that they planned and conducted. A large number of officers reached the rank of brigadier-general, the most junior general's rank, and every division was commanded by a major-general, so thousands of officers held senior rank. Above the rank of major-general they thinned out. Even so, over the period of the war many officers in the Allied armies held the rank of lieutenant-general or its equivalent.

Lieutenant-generals commanded corps and sometimes armies, though usually an army was under a full general. Few field marshals – the French equivalent was marshal – existed until 1918, or until after the war, when most of the army commanders were promoted to that rank.

Considering the many hundreds of generals in service, few were outstanding by appraisals of the time or in hindsight. By outstanding, I mean innovative, enterprising and imaginative. To be fair, it was difficult for a divisional commander on the Western Front to be enterprising because he was constrained by tactics imposed by higher command.

A major-general had to do what he was told by his corps commander, who was under instructions from his army commander. And all of them were profoundly influenced by their commander-in-chief, whom they wanted to impress. Sycophancy was the key to success. The rank of brigadier-general disappeared before the Second World War, when officers of this level were merely brigadiers.

On many occasions a major-general commanding a division profoundly disagreed with the orders given him by his superior but he was in no position to change them. Some divisions were considered 'good' and some 'bad' but these gradings were the result of varying levels of morale and fighting spirit rather than of what they achieved. Brigadier-generals and major-generals could have a great effect on morale. The brigade commander or divisional commander who showed himself at the front and took the trouble to visit his men in their camps generally built up a strongly motivated force under his command.

Most soldiers of all armies never set eyes on an officer above the rank of brigadier-general. During my researches, over a period of many years, I always

Major-General John Russell, who commanded the New Zealand Division throughout its time on the Western Front, is little known outside his own country but his division was one of the finest in the entire Allied armies. The stature of the men he is inspecting is impressive.

asked old soldiers up to the rank of sergeant if they saw their own general. Perhaps two or three had done so. Most British soldiers had seen their own unit's commanding officer, generally a lieutenant-colonel, only on the occasion of a unit parade. The situation was different in Australian, Canadian and New Zealand units where the CO often visited his men, right down to platoon level.

Under General Sir John French, the first commander of the British forces in France and Belgium, and then under General Sir Douglas Haig for the remainder of the war, lesser generals rarely risked taking a chance to shine because the two commanders-in-chief might have seen them as potential rivals. Neither of these two ego-ridden men would have brooked competition.

Smith-Dorrien was considered an able general, even a clever one, and French got rid of him. Under Haig, the men who rose to command armies were Plumer,

General Sir Edmund Allenby, GOC of the British Third Army, before he was sent to take over all British and Empire forces in the Middle East.

Horne, Birdwood, Gough, Byng, Allenby and Rawlinson. Not surprisingly the ebullient, strong-willed Allenby was transferred to the Middle East. None of the others was conceivably a threat to Haig.

John Monash, commander of the Australian Corps after its formation in 1918, was the general who showed most imagination and initiative. It has long been said that Prime Minister Lloyd George wanted to dismiss Haig and replace him with Monash but this was never seriously considered. Monash held the rank of lieutenant-general only from mid-1918 and he was a citizen soldier,

not a regular soldier. With the British Army as rigid as it was in 1914–18, Lloyd George could not have jumped Monash over the shoulders of the several full generals senior to him.

In the French Army some generals commanded respect for their ability and courage but they had no more enterprise and initiative then their British confrères. Rigid in their outlook, they were operating to a strategy and tactics which had been valid a generation earlier. Joffre was as solid as a rock and no more enlightened; Pétain had the spirit of a great commander but he lacked the intellect of a Napoleon; Gallieni had ideas – he sent reinforcements to the front in Paris taxis at a time of crisis – but no overall view of the strategy required to fight a great war; Foch was incisive, a great quality, and he was the best of the French generals, but he seemed unable adequately to coordinate the movements of the vast numbers of men under his command in 1918.

The American commander-in-chief, General John Pershing, and his senior subordinate generals were ready to learn but, like their eager men, they made mistakes while they were doing so. They were overconfident but they had a keen intelligence, and had the United States entered the war earlier the American generals would have become prominent.

The German generals were highly professional and they showed more elasticity of thought than most of the

The Kaiser, surrounded by his staff officers, speaks to a British brigadier whose troops had been defeated and captured in a battle at Chemin-des-Dames in 1917.

Allied leaders. German students of the fighting on the Western Front have always stated that their generals *deserved* to win the war because they were so much cleverer than those of the Allies. At his superior level of command, Ludendorff was the great thinking general of the war. Max von Gallwitz and General Prince Rupprecht were able and incisive and they handled their formations skilfully. Some other generals were retained by the German general staff beyond their level of competence and thus made serious errors. But this also applied to the opposing armies. Haig should have been removed from command after the disastrous early failure of the Battle of the Somme. It was a feature of the First World War that failed senior generals were retained in their posts, often because of their political influence at home. Also, powerful generals on the staff at home, as well as politicians of cabinet rank, hesitated to sack generals in the field because they feared that such a step would reflect badly on them.

BULLARD, LIEUTENANT-GENERAL ROBERT LEE

Bullard graduated from West Point in 1885 and by 1917 he was a brigadier-general. In June that year he was appointed commander of the Second Brigade of the Third Division and took it to France. As a major-general he was given the American First Division in December and the following May he carried out the successful attack at Cantigny. A popular field commander, Bullard was promoted to command III Corps in July 1918 and he led this formation in the bloody fighting at the Vesle river or 'Death Valley'. These operations were part of the Allied counteroffensive along the Aisne–Marne

General Bullard, commander of the United States Second Army.

front after Ludendorff's 'Michael' Offensive petered out in July 1918. After leading III Corps to the Meuse–Argonne sector, Bullard took charge of the American Second Army on 12 October. During the final weeks of the war his sector was quiet.

BÜLOW, GENERAL KARL VON

An able infantry general, Bülow was given command of the German Second Army on 2 August 1914 and was responsible for the capture of the Belgian fortresses of Liège and Namur. These triumphs led to his being given nominal command over General von Kluck's First Army. His troops defeated the French Fifth Army on the Sambre river and Bülow had further successes at St Quentin.

The apparently invincible Germans crossed the Marne on 4 September but a 30 mile gap opened up between Bülow's Second Army and Kluck's First. Bülow showed the limitations of his thinking. When he realized that the French-British allies had discovered this gap Bülow panicked and showed all the symptoms of military paralysis. A staff colonel, arriving at Bülow's HQ on 9 September, recognized Bülow's inadequacy and ordered an immediate retreat from the Marne behind the Aisne river. Briefly, Bülow commanded the entire German right wing of three armies and on 10 October he took over a newly formed Second Army at St Quentin. In preparation for sacking Bülow, the Kaiser promoted him to field marshal in January 1915, following which he suffered a heart attack. The German general staff did not again offer him a command and in June 1916 Bülow resigned from the army.

BYNG, GENERAL SIR JULIAN

Byng was in Egypt when war broke out and was recalled to take command of the Third Cavalry Division, which he led during First Ypres. In March 1915 he commanded the Cavalry Corps but was sent to Gallipoli to take charge of IX Corps in August 1915. In May 1916 he was back on the Western Front in charge of the Canadian Army Corps. With this

A contemporary portrait of General Sir Julian Byng, GOC of the British Third Army.

corps, Byng checked a German advance in June at Mont Sorrel and Sanctuary Wood but with great loss of life among his own men.

In 1917 the Canadian Corps captured Vimy Ridge, a triumph for Byng and the reason for his being given command of the Third Army when Allenby was sent to the Middle East. In this capacity he planned the Cambrai Offensive. In November 1917, using 486 tanks as his spearhead, Byng was initially successful but the campaign failed for lack of infantry and reserves. Byng blamed the setback on his troops, 'namely,' as he said, 'lack of training on the part of junior officers and NCOs and men'. The Germans' Michael Offensive in March 1918 hit the Third Army but Byng, after losing the Cambrai Salient, held the enemy at Arras. With the Fourth and Fifth armies he drove the Germans back to the Hindenburg Line during a counter-offensive that began on 21 August.

CASTELNAU, GENERAL NOEL DE

More important on the Western Front than British histories indicate, Castelnau commanded the Second Army when the war began and moved it into German Lorraine in line with Plan XVII, which he had drawn up. On 20 August 1914 he was defeated at the Battle of Morhange but he managed to save the great fortress city of Nancy. In mid-1915 he commanded the central front and later that year he controlled the Champagne Offensive. When the Germans attacked

Verdun in February 1916, Castelnau was sent there and it was he who made the decision to defend to the last the great fortress complex. When Joffre was removed as commander-in-chief, Castelnau, who had been Joffre's chief of staff in 1915, also lost his job. In 1918 Foch gave him command of the Eastern Army Group in Lorraine and Castelnau successfully directed the final campaign there. An underestimated Western Front general.

FALKENHAYN, GENERAL ERICH VON

A lieutenant-general in 1914, the Prussian Falkenhayn fancied himself as a strategist. On 3 September 1914 he advised the chief of the general staff, General von Moltke, to capture the Channel ports and halt the German advance on the Marne. Von Moltke rejected the sound advice and two days later the hurried retreat from the Marne began. Moltke's reputation was lost and on 14 September Falkenhayn replaced him. He presided over the battles of attrition in October and November, mainly at Ypres. Just why he used units of raw recruits when he had veterans resting between the Aisne and the Vosges has never been clear. On 21 February 1916 it was Falkenhayn who ordered the great assault on Verdun. The German losses here, as well as a German rout on the Eastern Front, lost Falkenhayn his reputation and strengthened his enemies, who included Ludendorff and Hindenburg. He lost his job on 29 August 1916 and had nothing further to do with the Western Front.

FAYOLLE, GENERAL MARIE-EMILE

As an artilleryman, Fayolle saw that the French Army had too few guns in comparison with the German forces and he criticized Foch and Joffre, the French commanders of 1915 and 1916, for their wasteful infantry assaults. As commander of the Sixth Army he was responsible for the French part of the Somme Offensive in July 1916 and his advance greatly outstripped that of his British allies to the north. Nevertheless, he was considered too cautious and was transferred to command of the First Army, an inferior command, in 1917.

General Nivelle took over the Sixth Army and failed lamentably in an offensive of April 1917. When General Pétain became commander-in-chief he appointed Fayolle to command Centre Army Group. After a success at Verdun in August he was sent to Italy to be deputy commander of the French troops there. Back in France in March 1918, he was given command of forty divisions, but from then on suffered from conflicting orders and demands by Foch, now the Allied supreme commander, and by Pétain, the French commander-in-chief. Nevertheless, he performed well and during the summer of 1918 he controlled fifty-five divisions, fully half the strength of the French Army.

FOCH, GENERAL FERDINAND

With a diverse military background, the aggressive Foch quickly gained promotion in the first months of the war

A 1916 postcard showing, from the left, General Joffre, President Poincare, George V, General Foch and General Haig.

and by December 1914 he held power second only to that of Joffre, the commander-in-chief. He was responsible for wasteful offensives in Artois during May and September 1915, but learned from these reverses. At the end of 1915 Foch reported that a decisive break-through was a responsible action; the reality of trench warfare demanded that the Allies should make attacks on various parts of the front and wear down the Germans. His own attack on the Somme was not successful and when Joffre was sacked in December 1916, to be replaced by General Nivelle, Foch fell with him.

For fully a year Foch was more a consultant but he was made chief of the general staff after Nivelle's fall from grace. When the Germans launched their offensive in March 1918 coordination of

A rarely seen photograph of General Foch. The enormous pressures of command over the entire Allied force show on his lined face. The undone uniform pocket perhaps hints at his preoccupation.

Allied operations became vital and Foch was given this task. On 3 April he was given the authority for the 'strategic direction' of the armies and on 14 April he was named Supreme Allied Commander-in-Chief. At first this meant control over French, British and American forces but soon he had similar authority over the Italian and Belgian forces as well.

The Allies somehow absorbed the power of the German attacks, which lost their power by July. Foch then organized the Allied offensive that was maintained until the victory in November 1918.

FRENCH, FIELD MARSHAL JOHN DENTON PINKSTONE

French was nearly sixty-two when he was given command of the British Expeditionary Force on 4 August 1914. He landed at Boulogne on 14 August and on the 23rd his formations were in action at Mons. Virtually enveloped, the BEF retreated. French was too far from the front and he panicked, ordering a retreat from Mons. The Secretary of State for War, Lord Kitchener, hurried to France and countermanded the order to retreat. French blamed General Smith-Dorrien, commander of II Corps, for the setback.

French led the BEF to Belgian Flanders and late in October he reported to Kitchener that the Germans were 'playing their last card' in Flanders. This was a wildly optimistic forecast. He made another error of judgement in March 1915 when he tried to break the Germans' lines at Neuve Chapelle and the British suffered

A rarely seen image of General Sir John French, commander-in-chief of the BEF for the first eighteen months of the war.

heavy casualties. Another disaster followed in April when the Germans counter-attacked. Driven by a mixture of desperation and overconfidence, French began an offensive in Artois on 25 September 1915, only to be repulsed twice; his troops again suffered heavily. After trying gas against the Germans at Loos, French broke off his offensive on 14 October and on 4 December he resigned, to be succeeded as commander-in-chief in France by Douglas Haig.

GALLWITZ, GENERAL MAX VON

Gallwitz arrived on the Western Front, from the Eastern Front, in March 1916 and was appointed commander of Meuse Group West at Verdun, but he soon moved to the Somme where he was chief of another army group. In December 1916 Hindenburg and Ludendorff gave Gallwitz the Fifth Army and ordered him to steady and then hold the sector. In January 1918 he commanded Army Group Gallwitz and in the Meuse–Moselle sector he confronted the American Army. His troops held the strong Michael Line and finally stopped the Americans' assault in the St Mihiel Salient. He ranks as one of the most able German generals.

GOUGH, GENERAL SIR HUBERT

In the first year of the war Gough was only a divisional commander, in turn commanding the Third Division, the Second Cavalry Division and the Seventh Division. Early in 1916 Haig gave him the command of I Army Corps and by mid-year he was commanding the new British Fifth Army – at the age of only forty-five. An impetuous leader, Gough demanded results regardless of the cost and he flung his divisions at the strong German positions on Pozières Ridge. After terrible losses the British, Australians and Canadians took the ridge and Gough ordered a pursuit of the Germans into the low ground east of the ridge, where the Empire troops spent a fearful winter.

Gough was involved in the July 1917 offensive in the Ypres Salient, when again he pushed his troops beyond their limit to capture high ground which yielded no

Lieutenant-General Sir Arthur Currie, commander of the Canadian Corps.

strategic or tactical advantage. By the spring of 1918 Gough and his Fifth Army were again manning the Somme sector when Ludendorff's Michael Offensive hit his front. Gough's formations retreated over the old battlefields in a near débâcle that was blamed on Gough himself and he was removed from command.

He is best remembered for the cavalier way in which he swept aside the objections of his best generals when they pointed out the dangers of his plans for frontal attacks.

HAIG, FIELD MARSHAL SIR DOUGLAS

When the war broke out Haig, as a lieutenant-general, commanded I Army

Field Marshal Sir Douglas Haig, commander-in-chief of the British armies on the Western Front. (*Illustrated London News*, 28 October 1917)

Corps, which he took to France as part of the BEF. Since he anticipated the German Army's march through Belgium, he was prepared for the retreat from Mons at the end of August. He was ordered south-west but instead headed south and thus exposed the flank of Smith-Dorrien's II Army Corps. This forced Smith-Dorrien to make a stand at Le Cateau. On 9 September Haig's I Corps took part in the French counter-attack and crossed the Marne. He could have separated the German First and Second armies but an inaccurate aerial report inclined him to caution. He did

cross the Aisne several days later but ran into strong resistance.

During First Ypres the robust defence of Haig's corps blocked four German corps. When the BEF was organized into two armies Haig was given the First Army, consisting of three corps. In March he attacked at Neuve Chapelle, in his own words, 'regardless of loss'. His men made several brave attempts to break through the German trenches in the face of machine-gun fire but failed completely. Haig still viewed the machine gun as 'a much overrated weapon'.

Haig's part in a great offensive in Artois in May 1915 was to storm Aubers Ridge. He failed to capture it and the entire operation was a failure. Following the next British failure – that of General French at Loos – Haig was appointed, on 19 December 1915, as Commander-in-Chief of the British and Empire Forces. Haig's secret despatches to King George V concerning the inadequacies of French's leadership had helped him into the supreme command.

The British had four armies in the Western Front by 1 July 1916, the formal date for the beginning of the Battle of the Somme. On the first day of this horrendous struggle of attrition the British lost 60,000 men, and before the offensive was called off in November the total casualties were 400,000. Haig and Joffre wanted to renew the attack but the British and French governments would not sanction their field commanders' plans.

General Haig, as painted by a French artist in May 1916.

In January 1917 Haig was required to support an offensive by General Nivelle, the new French commander-in-chief. This was another disaster. The British advance was on the Arras sector but the Germans had chosen to withdraw to the Hindenburg Line and Haig's movement met no opposition. At French insistence, Haig kept up the pressure on the German armies while the French Army was reorganized. While General Plumer attacked Messines with the British Second Army, Haig, on 31 July, launched Third Ypres (Passchendaele), a misery of a battle which cost the British and Empire troops another 400,000 casualties.

When the German offensive pounded the British lines on 21 March 1918 and caused a critical situation, Haig agreed to work under a French supremo, General Foch. This arrangement did not protect the British lines from further onslaughts and that on 9 April in Flanders near Neuve Chapelle was especially dangerous. The Germans broke up and in some cases routed British divisions. On 10 April Haig issued his famous Order of the Day: 'There is no other course open to us but to fight it out. Every position must be held until the last man. With our backs to the wall and believing in the justice of our cause each one of us must fight to the end.'

Following a great French counterattack on 18 July, Haig took the offensive. Beginning on 8 August, his armies attacked along the line of the Somme, fighting on the battlefields of 1916. Much has been made of Haig's generalship in the last months of the war but the end of German resistance was the result of factors that had nothing to do with Haig. They included the British naval blockade of Germany, the massive strength of the fresh American armies and political discord in Germany.

Herwig and Heyman have written a concise assessment of Haig as a commander: 'He was unimaginative, not receptive to creative inventions, refusing in 1915 to acknowledge the importance of the machine gun and cancelling construction of tanks. He displayed an obstinacy in adhering to fixed plans regardless of the facts pursuing unattainable goals, even at the price of destroying his own armies.'

HINDENBURG, FIELD MARSHAL PAUL VON

Hindenburg and his chief of staff, Ludendorff, were active on the Eastern Front and it was not until after 28 August 1916, when Hindenburg became chief of the general staff, with Ludendorff as his quartermaster general, that he became identified with the Western Front.

Very much a political figure as well as a military leader, Hindenburg became, in effect, a military dictator. He issued many decrees, most of which were actually written by Ludendorff. Hindenburg's name was given to the great German fortified defensive line that crossed France from the north-west to the southeast but he did not actually direct operations there.

In March 1918 the two generals decided on a massive assault near St Quentin, intending to break the Allied line where the

Directors of destiny: Hindenburg, the Kaiser and Ludendorff at Army HQ, probably in 1916.

British and French forces joined. They used fifty divisions between March and June and the German troops again reached the Marne, but the offensive had spent itself. During the Second Battle of the Marne Foch broke the German front by 8 August. Ludendorff resigned on 26 October and fled to Sweden.

Hindenburg was not the military genius which many people outside Germany suppose him to be, but his calm dignity gave him an aura of authority which was mistaken for intellectual power.

JOFFRE, MARSHAL JOSEPH JACQUES

When war broke out, Joffre was chief of the general staff. With his deputy, General Castelnau, he was the creator of Plan XVII, which defined French stategy should there be a war with Germany. In essence, it provided for a French thrust around Sedan should the Germans attack through Belgium. This became the Lorraine Offensive, which Joffre launched in mid-August 1914. However, under German pressure, Joffre was forced to withdraw his armies, but held firm on the Marne. After that one success he suffered a series of failures, which included Artois in May 1915 and Champagne in the September of that year. One of his great mistakes was to strip the Verdun fortresses of their heavy guns to support these offensives. By the

Two commanders-in-chief, Joffre and French. They are believed to have posed for this painting in the winter of 1914/15.

end of the year Joffre's inadequacies could no longer be tolerated and the prime minister, Aristide Briand, sacked him. Joffre is remembered as an unimaginative and rigid man but also one who was imperturbable during a crisis. This may have been his greatest weakness.

KIGGELL, GENERAL SIR LAUNCELOT EDWARD

For the first year of the war Kiggell served at the War Office, rising to be assistant to the chief of the Imperial General Staff. In December 1915 Haig, as newly appointed commander-in-chief, invited Kiggell, a close friend, to be his chief of general staff on the Western Front. This was an unfortunate appointment because Kiggell was not only an officer of limited ability but also a sycophant. Somehow he 'sold' Haig on the disastrous tactic of massive assaults of infantry in successive waves.

It was Kiggell too who pressed Haig to maintain the offensive in Third Ypres long after it was clear that the armies were irretrievably bogged in the Flanders mud. After the battle had ended, Kiggell visited the front and broke down from 'nervous exhaustion'. Worried voices had been agitating for his removal but Haig was loyal to his friend until January 1918, saying that he needed 'Kigg's help and sound advice'. He was made Lieutenant Governor of Guernsey, where he could do no more harm.

KLUCK, GENERAL ALEXANDER VON

As a colonel-general, Kluck commanded the First Army when war broke out and thus was responsible for the Germans' tremendous wheeling movement through Belgium. The operations were initially successful as Kluck's divisions enveloped Brussels, defeated the BEF near Mons and again soon after at Le Cateau. Kluck then made a fatal mistake. Instead of advancing southwards along the Channel coast and enveloping Paris, as the original plan demanded, he conceived the idea of fighting a new battle of Sedan (the first was in 1870) and wheeled his army east of Paris.

In this southward movement he defeated the French near Amiens but in the process exposed the flank of General von Bülow's Second Army. During First Marne, Kluck had another victory over the French Sixth Army when he was 'advised' by an officer from German field HQ in Luxembourg to pull back behind the Aisne. In effect, this retrograde movement gave the French the victory in the Battle of the Marne. Kluck was seriously wounded in the leg on 28 March 1915 and was retired soon after.

LIGGETT, LIEUTENANT-GENERAL HUNTER

As commander of the US First Army Corps, Liggett was largely the brain behind the reduction of the St Mihiel Salient in September 1918, the Americans' first major victory in the war. This success brought him promotion to

Lieutenant-General Hunter Liggett, a renowned American leader.

command of the American First Army in October and in the Meuse–Argonne Offensive his troops broke through the Hindenburg Line. This was done in force and caused the Americans heavy casualties, but by 6 November Liggett reached Sedan. Liggett's reputation rested on his understanding of the tactics necessary to defeat the Germans in 1918 and he was immensely respected in the American Army.

LUDENDORFF, GENERAL ERICH

When war broke out Ludendorff was deputy chief of staff of the German Second Army, under Bülow. On 8 August his rapid capture of the Belgian fortress of Liège brought him to prominence and he led the advance across the Sambre river. Transferred to the Russian or Eastern Front, Ludendorff spent the next two years away from the Western Front. His influence on the Western Front dates from 29 August 1916, when he was appointed the first quartermaster general of the German forces. Hindenburg was largely a figurehead and with the Kaiser politically occupied Ludendorff was de facto commander-in-chief.

It was Ludendorff who gave the orders for the building of the Siegfried Line, which the Allies gave the label of the Hindenburg Line. Ludendorff initiated the German-Austrian campaign against Italy and its allies in October 1917 and inflicted 600,000 casualties at the Battle of Caporetto. He was also responsible for the great Michael, Mars, St George I and St George II operations in the west in 1918, and by the end of May his troops had punched three immense salients into the Allied lines.

One of Ludendorff's few failings as a great commander is that he had not appreciated the potential of the tank; thus the British tank attack east of Amiens on 8 August startled him. It was he who described that occasion as 'the black day of the German Army', though the 30,000 troops he lost that day were relatively few when compared with the French and British casualties in many battles.

Losing confidence in Germany's ability to win the war, Ludendorff at first recommended that the nation make peace. Then he changed his mind and wanted to fight on. Prince Max von Baden saw Ludendorff as confused and weak, and forced his resignation on 26 October. Ludendorff was one of the great leaders of the war, both as a strategist and tactician. However, despite his energy and capacity he had serious limitations, especially of imagination and political understanding. All Allied troops fighting on in France and Belgium – the Western Front of 1918 – were in effect fighting Ludendorff so he has a special place in the Front's history.

MANGIN, GENERAL CHARLES

A forthright general, Mangin expected much of his troops but they had no affection for him. Among his achievements was the recapture of Douaumont, Verdun, in October 1916, when he took 7,000 prisoners. A supporter of General Nivelle, Mangin was appointed to command the Sixth Army but even his help did not save the Nivelle Offensive from failure. Nivelle then unfairly blamed Mangin for the failure. Foch gave him command of the Tenth Army in 1918 and with it Mangin attacked the west flank of the salient in the Second Battle of the Marne, July 1918.

MONASH, LIEUTENANT-GENERAL SIR JOHN

An Australian, Monash had been prominent during the Gallipoli campaign of 1915 and reached the Western Front in 1916 as a major-general commanding the

General Charles Mangin, a fire-eating French general who was unpopular with his troops.

AIF Third Division. His reputation as a planner and organizer grew following his part in the Battles of Messines, June–July 1917, and the subsequent Battle of Passchendaele (or Third Ypres) in the latter half of 1917. In May 1918 he replaced General Sir William Birdwood as commander of the Australian Army Corps and began the most momentous period of his military life. The planning for the highly successful Battle of Hamel, on 4 July, was

Lieutenant-General Sir John Monash, commander of the Australian Corps, presenting a decoration to a soldier of the AIF 2nd Division. (Australian War Memorial)

entirely his and he conducted the AIF's advance on 8 August with outstanding skill. Monash followed these triumphs with the capture of Mont St Quentin and Peronne on 1–3 September. There followed the significant role of the AIF in the offensive against the Hindenburg Line; Monash wrote that his tactics were 'to advance [his] infantry under the maximum possible protection of the maximum possible array of mechanical resources'. For instance, during the Battle of Hamel he ordered that tanks would advance with the infantry rather than ahead of them. While his tactics and regard for the lives of his men were commendable, Monash was so proud of his Australians' skill and courage that he pushed his weakened units too hard in September–October 1918.

NIVELLE, GENERAL ROBERT

Nivelle was only a colonel of artillery at the outbreak of war but his dynamism turned him into a major-general and commander of the French Second Army in the spring of 1915. He was the creator of the 'creeping barrage', a term which frequently occurs in records of the war. Continuous shellfire pinned down the enemy while French infantry advanced behind its protection. In October that year, with General Mangin, he recaptured the great fortress of Douaumont and became a household name.

Just two months later he was appointed French commander-in-chief in succession to Joffre. Promising the politicians rapid success, Nivelle planned an enormous offensive, in which the British role was an attack at Arras. His eloquence and confidence broke down all opposition to his plans. Nivelle allowed for 10,000 French casualties on the first day, 16 April 1917. He suffered 100,000 casualties and the attack broke only part of the German first line. After only four days his splendid vision was in ruins and he settled for the strategy of attrition which he had so strongly denounced. Because of Nivelle's public stature he could not instantly be dismissed, but mutinies were breaking out and soon he was induced to hand over his command to General Pétain.

He appeared before a military court which, to protect other reputations, cleared him of serious misconduct. He was transferred to North Africa, a virtual banishment. The Nivelle Offensive, as it was called, nearly destroyed the French Army.

PERSHING, GENERAL JOHN

When Pershing was given command of the American Expeditionary Force on 26 May 1917, he took with him to the Western Front only one presidential order: 'Retain independence of command.' Since he considered the French and British generals incompetent, Pershing resisted when they urged him to amalgamate his units with those of their experienced allies, so that they could learn trench warfare. Instead, Pershing trained his men for open warfare.

General Nivelle, whose offensive in 1917 was a total disaster.

General Pershing, the American commander-in-chief, in his tent in the summer of 1918.

General Tasker H. Bliss, one of Pershing's top men.

However, certain units did later train with the Australians and French.

The Americans fought at Cantigny, Château-Thierry and Belleau Wood but Pershing was eager for a purely American victory. He had this opportunity at the St Mihiel Salient in September 1918, and as the Germans had begun to withdraw their troops the night before, Pershing's troops joined in the general advance against the Hindenburg Line. Pershing's great success as a general was his insistence on sound preparation and on logistics.

PÉTAIN, MARSHAL HENRI PHILIPPE

In 1914, at the age of fifty-eight, Pétain was approaching retirement age and he commanded only a brigade. However, he quickly made his mark and in September he commanded a division and by October the XXXIII Corps. A profound believer in the continuous use of artillery, he made progress during battles that his colleagues could not match. He performed so well in the Artois Offensive, which was otherwise a failure, that he was given command of the Second Army. The troops trusted him since he made it clear that he preferred to waste shells rather than lives.

Pétain was ordered to hold Verdun no matter what the cost and it was he who declared, 'Ils ne passeront pas', probably the most famous slogan of the war. He at

General Henri Philippe Pétain, second only to Foch in his influence on the French Army during the war.

chief. The job went instead to Nivelle, whom Pétain replaced after the disastrous Nivelle Offensive. His first task was formidable – to restore the morale of the French Army. To do this he personally visited ninety divisions and promptly introduced better conditions for the men. Under his guidance, competent generals improved French battle tactics. Pétain had to play second fiddle when Foch was made Allied supremo in April 1918. After initial difficulties the two men cooperated well and productively. Pétain was one of the few senior Allied generals to demonstrate imagination, humanity – despite his insistance on some mutineers being executed – and foresight. Above all, he understood how to fight the new kind of war.

PLUMER, GENERAL SIR HERBERT
Aged fifty-seven in 1914, Plumer was already a lieutenant-general, and in December that year he commanded II Army Corps. He was in charge of this army and of operations in the Ypres Salient throughout the period 1915–17. He was responsible for the Battle of Messines, which began on 7 June 1917, when nineteen huge mines exploded under the German trenches, and he captured the Messines–Wytschaete plateau with only a fraction of the casualties predicted by Haig's GHQ.

Following the costly start to Third Ypres (Passchendaele) on 31 July, Haig transferred command from Gough to

once took the French artillery under his direct command and completely reorganized the positioning of the guns. Equally important, he gave the directions which led to Verdun being adequately supplied, a massive success in logistics. He also ordered that units serving there should be rotated systematically, a step that might have been dictated by military efficiency but was nevertheless humane. At great risk to himself he often visited the front, earning the respect of the rank and file.

For successfully defending Verdun he should have been made commander-in-

Plumer, and under his command the ground was eventually captured. Just before the 'official' end of the battle, Plumer was sent, on 9 November, to take charge of the British-French force sent to help the Italians on their front. Returning to the Western Front, Plumer took over command of the Second Army just before the Germans' Michael Offensive of 21 March 1918. The sectors he had been instrumental in capturing, Messines, Wytschaete and Passchendaele, were all retaken by the enemy. Nevertheless, Plumer remained steady, unlike some other Allied commanders, and he had the satisfaction of seeing the German thrust exhaust itself. When the final Allied advance began Plumer led the Second Army and in November crossed the Rhine. Certainly the most popular British commander, Plumer was also one of the best. Since he was junior to Haig he could not avoid participating in Haig's strategy of attrition, but he abhorred it.

RAWLINSON, GENERAL SIR HENRY
In 1914, at the age of fifty, Rawlinson commanded two divisions which covered the retreat of the Belgian Army after the Germans captured Antwerp. When he linked up with the BEF Rawlinson, a major-general, was given command of IV Corps, part of Haig's larger command. His formation took part in the battles of Neuve Chapelle, Aubers Ridge, Festubert and Loos. At the end of 1915 he was appointed to command the Fourth Army as a lieutenant-general.

A believer in attacks with limited objectives, Rawlinson had to follow Haig's decision to attack across the whole of the BEF's Somme front on 1 July 1916. The loss of nearly 60,000 men on the first day and about 400,000 in all by 18 November fell largely on Rawlinson's army. Promoted to general in January 1917, he planned a combined operations assault on the German-held Belgian coast but it never took place. Instead he found himself commanding the British left flank during the latter half of the Battle of Passchendaele.

In March 1918, in the wake of the destructive German Michael Offensive, he was given the shattered Fifth Army and ordered to reorganize it after Gough's removal from command. The hastily reinforced Fifth Army became the Fourth Army. His Australian troops captured Villers Bretonneux on 25 April and in doing so ended the German push. It was Rawlinson's Fourth Army which attacked along the line of the Somme on 8 August, an offensive which took Cambrai, Peronne and St Quentin, and advanced more than 60 miles. The war ended at this point. Rawlinson was one of the more enlightened British generals but he suffered from being heavily involved in Haig's strategy of attrition.

RUPPRECHT, FIELD MARSHAL AND CROWN PRINCE OF BAVARIA
Rupprecht was not a general merely because of his royal status; he was also a highly professional military leader. Only

forty-two when he was given command of the German Sixth Army, he was in the thick of the fighting against the French from August 1914. He then led his army on the Somme, at Arras and in the Ypres sector, in the Battle of Neuve Chapelle, March 1915, and at La Bassée and Arras. In July 1916 he was promoted to field marshal and in this exalted rank he became commander of three entire armies, grouped as Army Group Crown Prince Rupprecht. Throughout 1917 he feuded with Ludendorff over strategy and political objectives.

No arrogant warlord, Rupprecht understood the limitations of his soldiers.

He did not approve of the Michael Offensive of March 1918, but nevertheless he competently handled his armies and it was largely owing to his operations that the offensive was so successful for so long. Later he complained to the German chancellor, Count von Hertling, that it was pointless to prolong the war, but when he was overruled he soldiered on out of loyalty to his troops throughout the German withdrawal and until the Armistice. The Bavarian royal line ended with the abdication of Rupprecht's father, Ludwig III, and Rupprecht never contemplated its restoration.

CHAPTER THREE

THE ARMIES

The armies that fought on the Western Front were not only different in nationality but in their structure and training, and especially in their leadership. This was only to be expected in, say, a comparison between the British and German armies, but it applied also among the armies from the British Empire, notably Australia, Canada, New Zealand and South Africa. While they conformed to the same rank system and while the troops were given the same basic training, the armies were different in their attitude to the conduct of warfare.

All the Empire armies came under the command of a British commander-in-chief and the disposition of their armies was controlled by General Headquarters. It might have been expected that the troops of the Empire would increasingly adapt themselves to British practice. In fact, the opposite happened. They became more individualistically Australian, Canadian and New Zealand. This particular division was a model formation, superbly led and consistently well administered. It was sometimes badly used but this was because its GOC, A.H. Russell, a mere major-general, did not have the seniority to insist that certain operations which his division was expected to carry out were ill-judged.

The American Army was nominally part of the Allied force from April 1917 but its troops took no active part in operations until the middle of 1918. This army was always handicapped because it lacked its own artillery and tanks; they had to be borrowed from its allies. Even in the short time that it fought on the Western Front, the American Army developed the logistical competence for which the US forces were to become famous in subsequent wars. That it lost so heavily in five months of war was due to inexperience and enthusiasm.

For the first two years of the war the French Army was the victim of its passion for *la gloire* – military glory. In bright uniforms of red and blue – excellent aiming marks for the enemy – they bravely charged and bravely died in heaps. It was not difficult for the Germans to fulfil their intention to 'bleed the French Army white' because the French generals kept on massing their regiments for ever more frontal attacks. In any case, the French throughout the war had a longer front to maintain than their allies did. Like the Belgians, the French were fighting on their own soil; the British and Empire armies and the Americans were fighting on foreign ground.

The Germans, too, were at war on foreign soil – that which they had

Belgian infantryman, Victor Mourmand.

American officer, Lieutenant La Rue.

An Infantryman of the 37th Regiment.

A French infantryman.

Sergeant G.W. Kimberley, Royal Artillery.

An unnamed Scottish corporal.

A series from a contemporary publication of 1920, *Les Allies*, shows soldiers from the different forces.

C.E. Parker, Canadian.

Sergeant C.A. McChesney, NZEF.

Private Robert Hamilton, AIF.

Sergeant Parker R. Edward (or Edward R. Parker) of Coventry.

A Sikh under-officer.

An American sergeant.

invaded and occupied. The German Army was immense, capable of operating on two fronts at the one time, the Eastern and Western Fronts. It benefited from having a general staff that knew the business of war thoroughly, how to use railways and roads, how to convert the nation's industry to war production. The German Army was never short of weapons and ammunition, as the Allies were from time to time. The German Army also had extraordinarily high morale. Only divisions with this quality could have recovered within a day from the shocking experience of having nineteen great British mines decimate their ranks on Messines Ridge on 7 June 1917. Similarly, high morale brought them through the immensely heavy Allied bombardments and gave them the will to break the Allied lines in April–May 1918 and cause an ignominious retreat. Much of the German Army's strength came from the professionalism of its junior leaders, the courage and skill of its machine-gun corps and, in 1918, its innovative tactics.

THE BRITISH ARMY (BEF)

When the war began the British Army was small compared with the armies of the other powers because successive governments had believed that the Royal Navy would be adequate for any war that might develop in Europe. The navy would quickly defeat any combination of other navies and blockade enemy nations into submission, assisted by the British Expeditionary Force (BEF) of six infantry divisions and one cavalry division. These 150,000 professional soldiers were believed to be enough to do Britain's share in the European war to come.

The BEF, commanded by Sir John French, was to the left of the French line and here it fought delaying actions at Mons and Le Cateau before its engagement in the Battle of the Marne. In the first five months of the war, to the end of 1914, 86,237 men were killed or wounded. The BEF became famous for

Field Marshal Sir John French, a contemporary postcard.

A French artist's impression of cheerful British troops in a Flemish billet. Generally, families welcomed the British soldiers if only because the army paid for their board and lodging.

its steadiness and skill at arms, but it was inadequately trained in tactics.

As 1915 dawned, with troops in trenches along a 460 mile front, it was obvious that the war would be a long one. The French could not man the entire front and Lord Kitchener and the general staff assessed that the British would need an army of 2 million men to defend the 40 mile sector between Ypres and Givenchy. In fact, 1,186,350 recruits volunteered by the end of 1914, a remarkable response. The men of these 'New Armies' were enthusiastic but there was no prospect that they could be as well trained as the 'old' army. The

experienced, regular NCOs who might have instructed them had been wiped out during 1914.

Despite shortage of ammunition, especially of artillery shells, and of equipment, the army fought two offensives in 1915 – Neuve Chapelle and Artois–Loos. Both were failures and by the end of the year General French was removed from command, to be replaced by General Sir Douglas Haig.

Under Haig, the British Army, together with those of the British Empire, became committed to a war of attrition, with its attendant high casualties. In January 1916 the government introduced conscription to increase the number of battalions and to reinforce those weakened by battle. The Battle of the Somme, between July and November 1916, brought heavy casualties which virtually wiped out Kitchener's New Armies.

Haig's armies were engaged in three major and costly battles in 1917 – Messines, Third Ypres (or Passchendaele) and Cambrai. Messines and Cambrai began promisingly but in the end were as disappointing as Third Ypres. Unable to sack Haig for political reasons, the prime minister, Lloyd George, dismissed the chief of staff, Sir William Robertson, and reduced the number of men available for any further battles of attrition. However, under an agreement with the hard-pressed French, the British Army, with sixty divisions, extended its front in 1918 to confront a hundred German divisions.

The German offensive of March–May 1918 pushed back the British line and at times threatened to break it, but following massive reinforcement the Empire armies held and then attacked. With the support of more than 450 tanks, the attempt to recover the lost territory and end the war began on 8 August east of Amiens.

Following the breaking of the Hindenburg Line, the Allied armies pushed on into territory they had not before seen during the war. The British Army suffered 750,000 men killed, not including those incurred by the Empire armies, and another three million wounded.

Unlike the French Army, the British Army's operations were not affected by mutiny. However, at the great training base of Etaples, on the French coast south of Boulogne, a six-day rebellion occurred in September 1917. It came about as a result of resentment against the conditions and sometimes harsh discipline of the camps, which a few soldiers exploited. The trouble was contained and did not spread to the trenches.

THE AUSTRALIAN IMPERIAL FORCE (AIF)

The AIF had been on active service at Gallipoli and the Middle East generally and reached France in March 1916. The First and Second Divisions were the first formations to arrive, followed by the Fourth and Fifth. The Third Division, which was raised in Britain, came later. A total of 314,814 men embarked from Australia, including about 6,000 who had returned from the war and been discharged only to re-enlist and re-embark. This was a large number of men from a country with a population of less then four million in 1915.

For the first two years the AIF divisions were part of British corps and armies and thus, in major respects, they came under British command. A notable exception was capital punishment. The Australian government insisted throughout the war that no Australian soldier could be executed for any crime. It was the only national force to be so exempt.

A studio photograph, taken in England in 1915, of a Tommy in full marching order, complete with sheepskin vest.

An Australian soldier's artistic impression of one of his mates. With a play on words, John P. Davis shows the Somme battlefield as liquid mud in the winter of 1916/17. A soldier bearing rum jars, perhaps illicitly obtained, was a welcome sight.

The AIF's first battle was Fromelles, 19–20 July 1916. It also fought at many places during First Somme, notably Pozières, Flers and Gueudecourt. AIF divisions were also heavily committed in the Ypres Salient, at Messines, Polygon Wood, Broodseinde and Passchendaele. In France they fought the two battles of Bullecourt and several smaller battles in the Bullecourt area, including the two battles of Villers Bretonneux, as well as Lys River, Hamel, Mont St Quentin and Peronne, and another twenty battles before the Australians' final fight at Montbrehain on 4 October 1918.

On 31 May 1918 all five AIF divisions came under direct Australian command. Promoted to lieutenant-general, John Monash took over the new Australian Corps. In effect it was an Australian army, but with only five divisions it was not considered large enough to merit this title. The corps played a significant part in the final Allied operations of the war.

In the period from 27 March to 5 October 1918 the five divisions represented less than 10 per cent of the whole British and Empire forces on the Western Front, but they captured 23 per cent of the prisoners, 23.5 per cent of the enemy guns and 21.5 per cent of the ground wrested from the Germans.

The Australians who lost their lives number 59,330 in all theatres of war. Wounds received by Australians numbered 152,171; many soldiers were wounded more than once. These casualties amounted to 65 per cent, the majority of them occurring on the Western Front, where 179,537 Australians were killed or wounded.

The AIF was the only wholly volunteer army on the Western Front, although Kitchener's 'New Army' was made up of volunteers. Also, nearly all Australian officers reached their commissioned rank after service in the ranks. Some private soldiers rose to become colonels.

The Australians were constrained by the limitations placed on them by the rigid British High Command until spring 1918. From then on they were able to exercise their enterprise, notably in what they called 'Peaceful Penetration', surprise raids into the German lines. The AIF capture of Mont St Quentin is considered to be one of the great feats of the war.

THE CANADIAN EXPEDITIONARY FORCE (CEF)

Volunteer enrolment for the CEF began on 3 August, a day before Britain declared war on Germany, and the first contingent, commanded by Lieutenant-General E.A. Alderson, left for the war early in October. It consisted of units of the First Division and Princess Pat's Canadian Light Infantry, 30,000 infantry and 8,000 cavalry.

After training on Salisbury Plain and at Ruelles, near Le Havre, the Canadians went first to the Ypres Salient. They were attached to the British Second Army and were in trenches at Langemarck on 22 April 1915 when the Germans began Second Ypres with a gas attack. This caused casualties among the unprepared French Colonial Division to the Canadians' left and panicked them. The Canadians filled the breach and their brave behaviour there 'set the standard for the Canadian Army that was to be', as one of their early historians said.

Overall, Canada raised more than 500,000 men for the war, of which 80 per cent were fighting personnel. By 19 August 1916 the CEF had four divisions in the field. The intention was to form a fifth, as the Australians had done, but the Canadian government preferred to be able freely to reinforce the four already in existence. Nevertheless, during the 'Hundred Days' –

which began on 18 July 1918 – Canada resorted to conscription, unlike Australia.

The Canadian Corps was always attached to one or other of the British armies, and after its service on the left flank at Ypres was in the trenches along the St Eloi–Loos front on the right.

The cavalry units had already become infantry. Like the British earlier, the Canadians learnt that cavalry had no role in trench warfare. They fought on the Somme in the summer and autumn of 1916, capturing Pozières and Courcelette.

On 9 April 1917 they were the principal force in the capture of Vimy Ridge, a much fought-for prize. They achieved success largely because all units involved in the assault reached their start-line along tunnels dug through the chalk. They captured most of their objectives in a single day and the entire position four days later.

The Canadian Corps' principal operation in 1917 was in October, when it was thrown into the mud of Passchendaele to continue the assault begun by the British, Australians and New Zealanders. Some AIF infantry had penetrated to the crossroads in Passchendaele but the fresher Canadians captured the ruins of the village, at great cost.

The Canadian prime minister, Robert Borden, complained about the loss to Lloyd George, the British prime minister: 'The gain was not worth the candle, the result was not worth the loss.'

After involvement in the Battle of Cambrai on 20 November 1917, the CEF was holding a sector of the northern Western Front when the German Army launched its tremendous push in March 1918. The attack left the Canadian front untouched, which many Canadians considered a compliment to their reputation.

They helped in the battle of Villers Bretonneux in April and they were on the Australian right, south of the Somme, when the great Allied offensive began on 8 August. A Canadian soldier serving with the CEF wrote, 'The months of August, September and October gave us a new heaven and a new earth with our cavalry a familiar feature on the battlescape and our own air force flecking the blue.'

The Canadian Independent Force (CIF) of armoured cars and truck-mounted machine guns ranged far and wide over the battlefield and was able to keep in touch with Corps HQ by radio. The CIF was an enterprising idea, decades ahead of its time.

The CEF captured the Droccourt–Quéant line, the canals du Nord and Sensée, and Cambrai on 9 October. Mons fell to it on the morning of 11 November. About 60,000 Canadian men were killed and more than 100,000 wounded. The Canadian Corps' commander for most of the war's duration was Lieutenant-General Sir Arthur Currie, an able leader.

THE NEW ZEALAND EXPEDITIONARY FORCE (NZEF)

New Zealand offered the British government an expeditionary force on 5 August and it was accepted on 12 August. The Main Force, as it was called, sailed on 16 October under Major-General John Godley. The New Zealanders fought their first campaign, with the Australians as their comrades, at Gallipoli, and in April 1916 they reached the Western Front.

Never more than one division in strength – a large number of men for a tiny country – the New Zealanders took a full share of the fighting. The division was committed to the Somme Offensive in September 1916 and 1,560 were killed. With two Australian divisions, the New Zealand Division bore the brunt of the fighting at Messines in June 1917, losing 640 men and another 3,700 wounded. In October 1917 at Passchendaele the division lost 1,560 in the space of a few hours. It was small consolation that in suffering these losses the New Zealanders achieved a remarkable reputation as front-line soldiers.

W.F. Massey, prime minister of New Zealand, told the British prime minister, Lloyd George, 'The New Zealanders were asked to do the impossible and were shot down like rabbits.'

Many New Zealanders won decorations for exploits involving individual enterprise and initiative. Typical of them was Sergeant Dick Travis, who had a reputation as a night scout. Before July 1918 he had won the DCM, the MM and the Belgian Croix de Guerre. On 24 July he was in action at

A long line of British Guards on the march in 1915. (IWM Q69587)

Hébuterne, where he won the VC posthumously. His citation reads:

> During surprise operations it was necessary to destroy an impassable wire block. Sergeant Travis, regardless of personal danger, volunteered for this duty. Before zero hour, in broad daylight, and in close proximity to enemy posts, he crawled out and successfully destroyed the block with bombs, enabling the attacking parties to pass through. A few minutes later a bombing party was held up by two enemy machine guns and the success of the whole operation was in danger. Sergeant Travis, with great gallantry and disregard of danger, rushed the position, killed the crews and captured the guns. An enemy officer and three men immediately rushed at him from a bend in the trench and attempted to retake the guns. These four he killed single-handed, thus allowing the bombing party, on which we much depended, to advance. He was killed 24 hours later.

Training in 1916 for the Battle of the Somme, New Zealanders had been issued with the 'lemon squeezer' hats that made them as distinctive as the Australians. Both of them were known as Diggers and they addressed each other in this way.

The New Zealand Division's final battle was at Le Quesnoy, when the old city walls were scaled in order to capture the town. By 11 November 13,500 New Zealanders had been killed and 35,000 wounded. Another 3,500 were killed at Gallipoli or in the Sinai and another 6,000 wounded. All these casualties came from the total of 100,000 sent overseas. The casualty rate in proportion to the population was the highest in the Empire.

Some historians consider that the New Zealand Division was the finest British and Empire division to serve on the Western Front, and I consider Major-General Andrew Russell, GOC of New Zealand Division, to be the best all-round divisional commander.

THE AMERICAN EXPEDITIONARY FORCE (AEF)

The United States had no history of military involvement in Europe and a strong tradition of isolationism; that is, keeping out of foreign political and military entanglements. The nation was openly on the side of the Allies but its entry into the war was delayed until April 1917. Its small, poorly equipped army had then to be transformed in order to play a role in the gigantic battles of the Western Front.

General John 'Black Jack' Pershing, commander-in-chief of the US Army in France. A portrait by Leon Hornecker.

General John Pershing was appointed to command the AEF and arrived in Europe in June 1917. Having been to the front and after briefings from the French and British commanders, he calculated that he would need 3 million American soldiers, 1 million of whom should arrive within one year. The build-up was slow but thorough. Pershing exasperated his European allies by refusing to commit his men until, as he said, American action could be decisive. He irritated the French and British still further by his insistence that the AEF must operate independently. Having been horrified by the inadequacy of the Allies' leadership, he did not want to entrust his men to leaders whose strategy and tactics had produced millions of casualties. The Germans' crushing victories of March and April led Pershing to be more flexible, but even so the American First Army was not created out of the AEF until July 1918.

In May 1918 the AEF had taken part in battle for the first time and captured Cantigny. In July, to gain further battle experience, it fought with the veteran Australians on the Somme, notably at Hamel on 4 July. The AEF had further successes at Château Thierry and Belleau Wood, and the force was engaged in the Second Battle of the Marne. The first wholly independent AEF battle came in September when it eliminated the Germans' salient at St Mihiel. In the Meuse–Argonne Offensive the AEF made slow progress, but when the massive force was reorganized into two armies the pace of advance was faster. Despite its late arrival in the field, the AEF suffered more than 300,000 casualties. The figure need not have been so high but the Americans often allowed their enthusiasm and courage to override their better judgement, and made frontal attacks against well-protected, undamaged German lines. By the Armistice more than 2 million 'doughboys' had arrived in France. The knowledge that the Allies could now call upon an apparently limitless number of fresh, strong, well-equipped American soldiers was a major factor in convincing the Germans that they could not win the war.

Georges Scott's impression of a young American soldier, a 'Sammy', in 1918.

THE FRENCH ARMY

The early days of the French Army on the Western Front are a study in statistics. With impressive efficiency, more than 2 million men were moved to the front in 4,278 trains, proof of the general staff's skilful planning. In all, the army had seventy-six infantry divisions and ten cavalry divisions, but this total practically exhausted the nation's military potential, and the Germans had 40 per cent more manpower.

The French Army, in colourful blue and red uniforms, was completely dedicated to the offensive, an integral part of the philosophy of *la gloire*, which the French believed could come only

An interesting photograph, taken in 1918, of French front-line specialists. From the left: light machine-gunner; rifle grenadier; light infantryman and scout; bomber; and infantryman in full assault gear.

from the attack. The troops were given no training in defence and no design for trenches existed in training manuals. The fine 75 mm field gun, an attacking weapon, dominated French artillery.

In effect, at the beginning of the war the French Army attacked the attacking German Army, but was surprised by German intentions and outmanoeuvred. The 300,000 French casualties of the Battle of the Frontiers showed how ill-prepared the army was for modern warfare. It is a tribute to the leadership at this time that the army did not disintegrate.

During 1914 and 1915 the British could do little and the French bore the main burden of trench warfare. Even then, the emphasis was on attack, in an attempt to cut off the German's great salient into French land. The army would have gone on fruitlessly and expensively attacking but it was compelled to defend the massive fortress area of Verdun, where the German commander, Falkenhayn, proposed to 'bleed the French Army white'. He very nearly succeeded but the defenders held out.

A French mother and her daughter-in-law receive news of a soldier's death in action. (From a contemporary painting by Georges Scott)

When Joffre departed and Nivelle took over in command, the French returned to the headlong offensive, regardless of the cost. Nivelle's Aisne Offensive in the spring of 1917 was a calamity. The French soldiers, shocked by the carnage and aware that their leaders saw them as nothing more than cannon-fodder, became restless and finally, beginning on 29 April, mutinies occurred. Before Marshal Pétain restored order on 9 June more than 120 serious mutinous acts had taken place. Pétain had some sympathy with the unhappy men but he still insisted on court martials and on the inevitable death penalties. More than 23,000 mutineers were convicted and 432 were sentenced to death. Of these, only fifty-five were executed.

While all this was going on the French Army was incapable of serious operations, and had the German High Command's intelligence been as efficient as it usually was, the German Army would have hit the French front with all its resources. Under Pétain's guidance the army reverted to a general policy of defence while its morale was rebuilt.

When Foch became supreme commander of the Allied armies he could confidently use the French divisions in the campaigns

Some insignias of French Army transport sections.

King Albert personally led the Belgian Army with Lieutenant-General Chevalier de Selliers de Moranville as his chief of general staff. Reorganized, the army remained unwieldy in structure until a further major reorganization in 1917 when it acquired the efficient French Chauchat machine-gun. The infantry battalions, no longer dependent entirely on rifle power, became smaller and more flexible.

Remarkably for a small population in a largely occupied country, Belgium mobilized 270,000 men during the war and maintained a frontline strength of 170,000. Its conscripts came from Free Belgium and from the men who had escaped to France and Britain. Casualties

of the summer and autumn of 1918. The French Army suffered grievously from inept strategy and tactics, losing 1,300,000 men and 4,200,000 wounded.

THE BELGIAN ARMY

Belgium believed that its three great fortresses of Antwerp, Nemur and Liège would keep it secure from invasion and 100,000 soldiers manned them in 1914. The German Army rapidly overwhelmed the forts but 18,000 Belgian troops from Antwerp crossed into Holland, preferring internment to capture. The remainder of the army withdrew in good order behind the River Yser, where it made a gallant stand and suffered 18,000 casualties.

Albert, King of the Belgians. Though not a professional soldier, Albert led his people in a truly martial manner and won the respect of his allies.

were heavy, with 44,000 killed and probably twice that number wounded.

In 1915 Britain supplied khaki cloth so that the Belgian troops could have a more serviceable wartime uniform than dark-red corduroy trousers, dark blue tunics and dark-blue or grey kepi.

King Albert was not always cooperative with his allies. In 1914 he declined to work with Marshal Joffre and in 1917 he refused to participate in the Allied 1917 offensive, saying that it would bring yet more devastation to Belgium. Belgian forces did cooperate in the final offensive of 1918 and Marshal Foch appointed Albert as commander of the Flanders Army Group, which included British and French units. On 28 September Albert led a British-French attack on a 23 mile front that recaptured 4 miles of territory, including Houthulst Forest.

Throughout the war the Belgian Army was responsible for the extreme left flank of the Western Front. Its soldiers fought bravely and a visit to a Belgian military cemetery is recommended. The headstones are strikingly distinctive because the national colours are part of their design. The easiest cemetery to visit is on the edge of Houthulst Forest, north of Ypres (Ieper) by the side of the N301. The role of the Belgian Army is often neglected in Western Front history; this cemetery is a reminder.

THE GERMAN ARMY

The peacetime strength of the German Army was 840,000 men, a large number indeed, but by December 1916 this army had more than 5.5 million men on service. They were divided into 2,200 infantry battalions, 550 cavalry squadrons, 2,150 field artillery brigades and 600 assault pioneer battalions. By the end of the war more than 13 million men had served in the German Army.

This was the basic infantry organization in the field:

A division had three regiments, each commanded by a colonel, with eighty officers and 3,200 other ranks. Each regiment had three battalions, each under a major, who led twenty-five officers and a thousand men. Each battalion had four companies, three of them infantry with one of machine-gunners, each led by a captain. Each company, led by a lieutenant, consisted of four platoons, each led by a corporal. At rock-bottom were the squads, two to each section, made up of eight men under a lance-corporal. The main contrast with British organization is that the Germans had fewer officers and much more responsibility fell on the NCOs. A sergeant-major often commanded a platoon and sometimes a company.

There was a strong German regular army but after it disappeared in 1914, as was the case with the British Army, the German Army became wholly conscript.

German youths became liable for conscription at the age of 17 and spent between two and three years in the army, after which they joined the reserve. This was no mere paper army; it was always active. In 1914 the army put eighty-seven

German infantry, 1914. The spiked *pickelhaubes* soon gave way to heavier, more protective helmets.

divisions into the field. The efficiency of the large regular reserve armies depended on career officers and NCOs, who had a fearsome reputation for tough competence. The army as a whole was a formidable fighting force, largely because of its magnificent general staff. Because of the generals' foresight and professionalism, the German Army was much better prepared for war than the Allies, especially in the quantity, quality and diversity of weapons. In addition, German industry was ready for war, especially with transport and ammunition. As far as is known, the army was never short of shells, as the Allies frequently were. Having long planned pre-emptive war to prevent the French and their allies from carrying a war into Germany, the Germans had no qualms about entering neutral Belgium.

Using seven of its armies, the general staff expected to win the war on the Western Front in six weeks, while providing only one army on the Russian front. The Austrian divisions did much of the fighting in the east.

Despite the competence of the general staff, it made two errors of intelligence assessment. It failed to assess the quality of the fighting men of the opposing armies and it was in error in supposing that its own armies could be equally successful on two fronts simultaneously. This problem bedevilled policy and strategy. Falkenhayn wanted to concentrate the major effort against France, while Hindenburg and Ludendorff pressed for decisive campaigns on the Eastern Front. As a result of Russian pressure against the allied Austro-Hungarian armies, Falkenhayn attacked the Russians in 1915 but did not defeat them. A simple statistic shows how the general staff was forced to divide its strength: in 1917 there were 2,850,000 troops on the Western Front, with 1,730,000 in the East. When the Bolshevik Revolution ended Russia's participation in the war, the general staff moved forty-four divisions to the Western Front.

After the Battle of the Somme the Germans rethought their defensive system. Until the end of 1916 they had favoured a continuous front line, but the High Command believed that this was responsible for high casualties. Under Ludendorff's direction, it decided on a lightly held series of outposts designed only to slow down and weaken an attack, and in the process disorganize it. To the rear of this outpost line was a main battle zone, up to 1½ miles deep, spiked with concrete strongpoints or blockhouses. Further behind the battle zone were many machine-gun posts and field artillery to deal with any enemy who managed to cross the battle zone.

Hindenburg and his planners theorized, as they worked out the new system, that when the enemy had overrun the outpost line the German guns would deluge it with shells to prevent reinforcements reaching their comrades by now attacking the strongpoints. Eventually, from the security of the artillery line, the German counterattack would be unleashed.

In mid-1917 Ludendorff went even further. He instructed that when the Allies began a barrage the German troops holding a line would be withdrawn. He pointed out to his subordinates that the enemy's shells would simply fall on unoccupied ground and make it increasingly difficult for the attackers to cross it. He believed that the pyschological impact on surviving British and French soldiers of dropping into an empty trench and almost immediately learning that they had to fight a still unscathed defence line would be immense. He was correct.

The German High Command adopted this system with the Hindenburg Outpost Line of fortified French villages protecting the Hindenburg Line itself. Enormous losses were inflicted upon the advancing Allied armies.

Simultaneously, the Germans introduced a new system of attack, modelled on the ideas of a French infantry officer who had been unable to convince his own superiors of its efficiency, and developed by General Oakar von Hutier. Perhaps it was just as well that the French officer was dead before the Germans put the system into practice.

A German gunner's observation post, built on a ruined house at St Eloi, 3 miles south of Ypres, August 1917. (Imperial War Museum)

The Germans raised stormtroop units of between two hundred and a thousand men, who, though heavily armed, would quickly advance, and under cover of smoke, terrain and natural vegetation, infiltrate the enemy lines of defence. In the meantime, these lines would have been pounded by German artillery.

Where the British or French held out stubbornly in pockets they would be bypassed and dealt with by German supports. The stormtroops would pass through the Allied rear, where they would attack gun positions whose crews would be already reeling from gas attacks. The Germans first used their new system to recover the ground lost to the British tank attack at Cambrai in November 1917. The most spectacular success came in March–April 1918 with

An enthusiastic send-off for German soldiers leaving for the Front. (IWM Q81779)

the German Spring Offensive, which sent the Allies reeling.

The Germans did not reinforce failure, as the British and French did until the end of the war, although some of the Allied manuals of the time warned against this practice. One of these manuals stated: 'More may often be accomplished by reinforcing a platoon which is not held up than by directly supporting one which is; the surest means of helping a neighbour in battle is to push on.' This was German doctrine as exemplified throughout the battles and campaigns of late 1917 and all of 1918.

In five great offensives in 1918 the German Army battered the old Western Front line out of shape. It used the most imaginative tactics of the war. The infantry advanced behind tremendous artillery bombardment and did not stop to overcome isolated pockets of resistance but flowed past them. That the German Army did not penetrate the Allied lines was due to logistical failures and the Allied reserve strength, particularly that of the newly arrived American divisions.

The German Army remained formidable while its supply of experienced senior NCOs lasted. When they dwindled away during the campaigns of attrition, the army's discipline and efficiency were weakened.

German soldiers skirmishing across a French field. Their helmets indicate 1916 or after but this field has neither trenches nor shellholes so the men may be training.

Significant differences existed between the various national segments of the German Army. For instance, Allied intelligence assessments considered that the Württemburgers were steadier in defence than the Bavarians, Saxons and others, while the Prussians were supposed to be more daring and dashing in attack. Whatever the validity of these judgements, it is undeniable that the fighting strength of the army as a whole depended on its splendid machine-gun corps.

CHAPTER FOUR

TO KNOW THE WESTERN FRONT, KNOW ITS LANGUAGE

It is not possible to know the Western Front without familiarity with the terms and abbreviations which are explained in this chapter. They are the army's language about itself, the war, the enemy and the Western Front. Men of all ranks used an argot and depended on terms and abbreviations that would have mystified the uninitiated civilian. When mixed with soldiers' slang – which could fill a book in itself – what the officers and men talked about was virtually incomprehensible to outsiders. For modern students of war on the Western Front it is essential to be able to understand, for instance, *daisycutter, Bangalore torpedo, Tickler's jam, toc emma* and all the other terms that the troops used in their everyday speech. This aspect of life on the Western Front has been too long neglected.

While this is an English-language list, I have also included those foreign-language expressions, especially French, which the British Empire armies generally understood and often used. In addition, there are a few expressions which might more correctly be used in a book of soldiers' slang but which, in this book, have a value in military history.

AA: *anti-aircraft, ack-ack, anti-aircraft fire*

AA&QMG: *Adjutant-General's branch and Quartermaster General*

abri: *shelter or dugout (from the French)*

abri caverne: *deep French dugout*

Ack Ack Ack: *full stop in telegraph message*

ack emma: *the morning (from am in phonetic alphabet)*

ADMS: *Assistant Director of Medical Services*

Adrian helmet: *French steel helmet, named after its designer*

ADS: *Advanced Dressing Station; after the RAP, the most advanced medical post*

AFO: *expression of disgust at quantity of paperwork (from 'Army Form Nought')*

A-frame: *wooden support shaped like a letter A, sunk upside down into the bottom of a muddy trench. A plankwalk rested on the crossbar of the A*

AHQ: *Army Headquarters*

Aid post: *synonymous with the RAP as the nearest medical post to the firing line*

AIF: *Australian Imperial Force*

Ak dum: *term for 'immediately' (from Hindustani). German noticeboards, which were often headed 'Achtung', were also ak dum*

ALH: *Australian Light Horse*

Alleyman: *British for a German (from the French Allemagne)*

Ally Sloper's Cavalry: *army name for Army Service Corps (from a character in the humorous paper,* Ally Sloper's Half-Holiday)

Amiens hut: *canvas on a frame used as a shelter in British base camps*

ammo: *universal British and Empire term for ammunition, especially SAA (q.v.)*

ammos: *slang for boots (from 'ammunition boot' – regular issue)*

AMS: *Army Medical Staff*

antennes: *light railways' main branches*

Antonio: *nickname for Portuguese troops*

ANZAC: *Australian and New Zealand Army Corps; often used in the plural*

AOC: *Army Ordnance Corps*

AP: *Aid Post*

archie: *anti-aircraft fire; also used as a verb (from a music-hall character)*

area shoot: *carpet shelling across an area of the enemy positions*

armlet: *brassard worn around the arm to indicate a particular duty, such as staff*

Armstrong hut: *collapsible hutlet of canvas and wood*

Army troops: *any unit attached to a division but outside brigade structure; performing line-of-communication duties such as road-making*

ARS: *French gas mask (Appareil Respiratoire Speciale)*

Asquith: *a French safety match as unreliable as Prime Minister Asquith's 'wait and see' advice on the war's progress*

AVC: *Army Veterinary Corps*

AWL: *Absent Without Leave*

AWOL: *(American) Absent Without Official Leave*

Ayrton fan: *a flag of canvas on a staff for dispersing gas when waved, named after the inventor*

BAB: *British telephone logbook after 1916 (also Bab code)*

Bangalore torpedo: *a length of piping filled with explosive, used to clear a way through wire entanglements but never very effectively*

banjo: *Australian for a spade*

Bantam divisions: *term for formations of British soldiers between 5 ft 1 in and 5 ft 4 in tall, called up when supply of taller men ran out*

barker: *a pistol; also a sausage (from the suspicion that army bangers contained dog meat)*

battle order: *infantry equipment reduced to the essentials, with the pack removed and replaced with the haversack*

battle police: *military police stationed behind an attack to intercept and check men moving back. Similar to the term battle stop*

BEF: *British Expeditionary Force*

belly: *a tank bellied when its underside caught on an obstacle and its tracks lost traction*

berm: *ledge on a trench parapet for storing ammunition and equipment*

BGGS: *Brigadier-General, General Staff*

BGRA: *Brigadier-General, Royal Artillery; usually the commander of corps artillery*

biff: *Bristol fighter plane*

Big Bertha: *any German heavy artillery but correctly the Big Bertha which shelled Paris. It was monstrous. With a charge of 550 lb of powder in a chamber 5 m long, it fired a shell with a 8.26 inch calibre. The gun fired only sixty-five times before being rebored. It was first fired on 23 March 1918. A total of 367 shells from several guns fell on Paris, killing 256 people and wounding 620*

Billjim: *Australian soldiers' term for themselves*

billy: *Australian cooking or boiling can*

blue-light outfit: *contraceptive pack issued at the Blue-Light Hut in the battalion lines*

boko: *slang for plenty or many (from French beaucoup)*

bomb: *hand grenade, and as frequently used as the term hand grenade*

bombardier: *Royal Artillery corporal*

bomb-proof: *proof against shell splinters*

bomb-stop: *traverse or obstacle in a trench to stop the attackers' progress*

bonk, to: *to shell*

bonzer: *also bonza, bosker and boshter, all meaning good or pleasing*

brass: *senior staff officers, from 'brass hat', so called because of the gold braid on their caps*

brassard: *armband or armlet*

breastwork: *a 'trench' built above wet or marshy ground. The front and rear walls were made of loose earth, sandbags, tree trunks and branches, masonry, smashed furniture and anything else to hand*

brigade: *the smallest tactical formation above a battalion, generally three or four battalions and support units*

British Warm: *heavy issue greatcoat for officers*

Brock's benefit: *many rockets and flares at night (from the fireworks manufacturer's name)*

buckshee: *free (from the Arabic baksheesh – tip)*

bullring: *training ground where recruits and convalescents were drilled for service at the front*

bundook: *a rifle, correctly bandook, (from Hindustani)*

bung: *cheese (from its constipating effect)*

burgoo: *porridge*

button-stick: *strip of brass with a central slot; when slid behind tunic buttons it kept the polish off the cloth*

buzzer: *portable telephone for tapping messages*

C3: *lowest British Army classification of*

fitness; men so listed were fit only for light duties at base

cable: *telephone landline usually run along a cable trench*

cadre: *selected officers and men held back when a battalion went into action, on whom their unit was rebuilt in the event of heavy casualties (see* **LOB***)*

cage: *prisoner of war holding depot*

camouflet: *the mining chamber and the mine itself used to blow up enemy mines*

canary: *instructor temporarily assigned from the front to base. These men wore yellow brassards*

cap comforter: *woollen stocking cap*

case-shot: *artillery shell for anti-personnel use; filled with steel balls, pellets, chain links*

cat: *nickname for a tractor, from the caterpillar tracks*

CCS: *Casualty Clearing Station; the main medical unit immediately behind the lines*

C de Guerre: *Croix de Guerre*

CEF: *Canadian Expeditionary Force*

CEP: *Portuguese Expeditionary Force (*Corpo Expedicionario Portugues*)*

CGS: *Chief of the General Staff*

CHA: *Commander Heavy Artillery; a corps appointment*

char: *general term for tea (from Hindustani)*

charger: *the metal clip holding five rounds for use in a magazine rifle, such as SMLE*

charpoy: *bed*

chats: *Australian soldiers' term for lice, which infested all front-line soldiers. Catching them and talking about them were frequent activities*

Chauchat: *French light machine gun*

chevron: *uniform distinction, but in British and Empire armies known as 'stripes'. Chevrons referred to service distinction and were worn on the lower right sleeve – red for 1914 service, blue for each succeeding year. Some soldiers wore gold chevrons for wounds*

Chinese attack: *fake attack. After the shelling ceased the enemy troops would man their trenches to repel the presumed attack; at this moment the artillery would resume the shelling and trap the defenders. 'Chinese' was used at the time to describe something flawed or false*

Chink: *slang for Chinese in the Chinese Labour Corps, whose men were often seen on the Western Front*

chit: *any note or written message*

chokey: *prison*

chub: *'Shut up!' or 'Be quiet!'*

CIGS: *Chief of the Imperial General Staff*

circus: *German air squadron, notably that of Richthofen; possibly from the large number of prominent tents from which each squadron operated or the bright colours the squadrons liked*

clink: *prison*

CO: *Commanding Officer; usually a lieutenant-colonel in command of an infantry battalion*

coal-box: *shell-burst causing a cloud of black smoke*

coffin-nails: *cigarettes*

communication trench: *any trench dug at an angle to the fighting trench and along which men and supplies moved*

con camp: *convalescent camp; a place much favoured because of its light duties*

concertina wire: *coiled barbed wire used in entanglements*

corduroy road: *temporary road surface made by laying cords of wood against one another across a path*

conchie: *conscientious objector*

cossack post: *advanced cavalry post or vedette*

covering party: *squad protecting a working party in no-man's-land or in the front line*

CP: *Collecting Post, generally for wounded or prisoners*

crabs: *lice (q.v.)*

crater: *the giant hole made by an exploding mine. The mine at Maedelstede Farm, Messines, contained 94,000 lb of explosives. That at Spanbroekmolen contained 91,111 lb and the crater still exists; it is 430 ft in diameter*

CRE: *officer commanding Royal Engineers; usually a divisional appointment*

creeping barrage: *artillery barrage moving forward systematically and at timed intervals to protect own troops during an advance*

crib: *bridge of metal and wood for tanks crossing branches or streams*

crump: *onomatopoeic term for shell-burst*

CSM: *Company Sergeant Major*

curtain fire: *barrage forming a 'wall' or curtain between a friendly unit and the enemy*

CT: *communication trench*

cushy: *much-used term for pleasant or likable, e.g. a cushy job at base*

DADMS: *Deputy Assistant Director of Medical Services*

DADOS: *Deputy Assistant Director of Ordnance Services; every division had a DADOS*

DAG: *Deputy Adjutant General*

daisycutter: *a shell that exploded immediately on contact with the ground; very dangerous for infantry men advancing*

DAQMG: *Deputy Adjutant and Quartermaster General*

daylight gun: *American troops' name for Benet-Mercié light machine gun, which they said could not be loaded in the dark. It could*

DCLI: *Duke of Cornwall's Light Infantry*

DCM: *Distinguished Conduct Medal*

DDMS: *Deputy Director of Medical Services*

decoration: *an award for exceptional bravery or service; for example, the VC, DSO, MC, DCM, MM. These decorations could be awarded more than once so that a recipient was then said to hold 'the MC and Bar'. The bar was of silver and graced the ribbon of the decoration. No soldier in British and Empire service actually wore more than one decoration of the same kind. A decoration was not, strictly speaking, a 'medal' (q.v.)*

dekko: *a look, usually a careful one*

demonstration: *a feint attack or bombardment*

Derby Scheme: *just before conscription was introduced in Britain, Lord Derby brought in a system of voluntary recruitment*

digger: *an Australian or New Zealand soldier. The term possibly comes from gold-miners of Western Australia or from Hamilton's order at Gallipoli to 'Dig, dig, dig!'*

dinkum: *Australian for good, true, authentic. A Gallipoli veteran was a 'dinkum'. 'Dinkum oil' was authenticated news*

dis: *disconnected; a break in telegraphic connection or to lose touch with a neighbouring unit*

ditch: *a tank was ditched when it could no longer proceed*

division: *the fundamental tactical formation, consisting of two or three brigades, together with supporting artillery, engineers and others*

dixie: *British camp kettle; later any food container*

DLOY: *Duke of Lancaster's Own Yeomanry*

DMT: *Director of Motor Transport*

Don R: *dispatch rider (from phonetic alphabet or signalese)*

doughboy: *nickname for American troops but originally a flour dumpling. Americans preferred this sobriquet to Yank or Sammies*

DOW: *Died Of Wounds*

draft: *reinforcements sent to a unit at the front*

drift: *deflection of a shell to the right, caused by the rotation from the rifled barrel*

drum fire: *an artillery barrage, which fired one gun at a time, like a drum roll. It was said to be disconcerting to those under it*

DSO: *Distinguished Service Order. The crude soldiery said that DSO stood for 'Dick Shot Off'*

duck board: *wooden planking in muddy trenches or across muddy ground. Without duck boards the armies would have been virtually immobile. A duck-board patrol moved on inspection at night along unmanned sections of the line*

dud: *a shell which failed to explode or anything that was useless*

duff: *primarily a pudding but also to duff a job or botch it*

dum-dum: *soft-nosed bullet or one with the nose scored across. These illegal bullets caused dreadful wounds*

ED: *Excused Duty because of minor illness or disability*

egg: *a bomb*

egg grenade: *a small German egg-shaped grenade*

elephant: *hut made from semicircular curved sheets of corrugated iron. Many dugouts were roofed with these 'elephant' sheets*

Emma Gee: *phonetic term for MG (machine gun); also Emma Gees, for the men of the MGC*

Emma Pip: *phonetic term for MP (military policeman)*

enfilade, to: *to fire along a trench from the end; not synonymous with flanking fire*

erk: *fitter of the RFC or RAF (from a contraction of air mechanic)*

ersatz: *German reserves*

estaminet: *café-bar on the Western Front where troops congregated*

exaspirator: *nickname for the box respirator*

FA: *Field Artillery or Field Ambulance. The letters also stand for 'sweet FA', meaning fuck all (from Fanny Adams or Sweet Fanny Adams, a murder victim)*

FANY: *First Aid Nursing Yeomanry; always pronounced 'fanny'*

fascine: *bundle of brushwood carried on tanks to fill trenches and ditches to permit tanks to cross*

FB: *British aircraft classification; Fighting Biplane*

FD: *Field Dressing.*

fernleaf: *for a while, a name for a New Zealand soldier, from his fernleaf cap badge*

feu pilote: French signal light

FFD: *First Field Dressing*

field dressing: *small pouch of bandage and iodine carried by each soldier for applying to a wound of his own*

field postcard: *this issue postcard carried several printed messages to be deleted as necessary. Field postcards were not censored*

fill: *the supplies necessary to make a tank battleworthy, generally 60 gallons of petrol, 20 gallons of water, 10 gallons of oil, and 200 6 pdr and 6,000 rounds SAA (for a male tank) or 10,000 rounds SAA (for a female tank)*

fire bay: *that part of a trench manned by the troops, ready to repel an attack*

fire step: *the step on the forward side of a trench upon which soldiers stood to observe or fire; the step was upwards from the trench floor*

fire trench: *front-line trench*

first reinforcements: *on coming out of battle the first reinforcements a battalion received were its own men in the cadre (q.v.)*

five-nine: *British term for a 5.9 in German shell*

Flammenwerfer: German flamethrower

flank barrage: *barrage directed against a flank, not from it*

fleabag: *sleeping bag*

flêchette: *dart dropped by one pilot onto another in combat*

flight: *the basic RFC unit of five or six aircraft*

flying pig: *mortar bomb*

FMO: *Full Marching Order; also FSMO, Field Service Marching Order*

FOO: *the Forward Observation Officer belonging to the supporting artillery*

forby: *rifle cleaning cloth (from 'four-by-two')*

fougasse: *a type of mine*

four-by-two: *a piece of flannel, white with red stripes, measuring 4 in by 2 in. It was placed in a loop on the 'pullthrough', the cleaning cord*

four-two: *British term for the German 4.2 in shell*

FF: *field punishment, the harsh punishment in which the soldier was tied to a gunwheel or stakes. He was also subjected to pack drill and a bread-and-water diet*

Fray Bentos: *corned beef of any origin, not just Fray Bentos brand*

frightfulness: *The troops' term for German behaviour, largely exaggerated*

Fritz: *general name for Germans; a diminutive of Friedrich*

front: *forward areas of operation in general*

funk hole: *a dugout; sometimes any protective hole. No funk was implied on the part of the officers and men who used a funk hole*

furphy or furphie: *Australian rumour (supposedly from the name of a garbage-cart operator in Melbourne)*

gasper: *cheap cigarette*

geese: *nickname for Portuguese troops*

GHQ: *General Headquarters*

girdle: *a tank's caterpillar tracks*

glasshouse: *army detention barracks or prison*

GOC: *General Officer Commanding, of a division*

gooseberry: *reel of barbed wire or entanglement; a reference to its prickles*

gorblimey: *field service cloth cap with the wire stiffening removed; a corruption of 'God blind me'*

greencross: *German gas shell; a reference to the mark painted on the shell*

greyback: *British Army shirt*

GS: *General Service, such as GS wagon*

GSO: *General Staff Officer; GSO 1 indicated General Staff Officer grade 1, usually a colonel*

GSW: *Gun-Shot Wound*

HAC: *Honourable Artillery Company*

hard tack: *army biscuit*

hate: *popular name for enemy bombardment*

Hauptmann: *German captain*

HE: *High Explosive*

Heinie: *American slang for a German*

heliograph: *a signalling instrument, using sun-flashes to send Morse messages*

homforty: *nickname for a French railway wagon (from the label on its side reading 'Hommes 40 Chevaux 8')*

hommes or **les hommes:** *French troops themselves preferred this description rather than* poilus *(q.v.)*

hop the bags: *leap over the parapet and move forward to attack*

horse lines: *where the transport was located*

hospital blues: *British convalescent soldiers wore a blue flannel jacket, white shirt, red tie and their unit headdress to indicate that they were patients. Innkeepers were supposed not to serve them liquor*

House: *the popular army game; later bingo*

housewife: *pronounced 'hussif'; the soldiers' pouch containing needle, thread, pins and a thimble*

howitzer: *a gun with a high, lobbing trajectory for shelling trenches and landing its shells behind enemy cover.*

Soldiers invariably called the weapon a 'how'

Hun: *common slang for German*

Huntley & Palmer: *RFC term for the twin Lewis guns mounted on some aircraft*

hush-hush: *anything secret or connected with intelligence*

hypo: *sodium thiosulphate, an antigas chemical*

I: *the intelligence section or branch*

iddy-umpty: *an army signaller, from the dot and dash of Morse code*

identity disc: *the name-tag bearing the soldier's number, unit and religion; made of composition, sometimes metal. From 1916–17 British Empire soldiers wore two. No. 1, green, remained on the dead soldier to identify the corpse on reburial; No. 2, red, was removed at the time of the original burial as proof of death. They were never known as dog-tags in the First World War but Australians called them dead-meat tickets*

igaree: *Australian for 'Hurry up!'*

imshi: *Arabic for 'Go away!'. Australian and British troops picked this up in Egypt*

iron rations: *a can of corned beef, tea, sugar and biscuit was carried by all soldiers but held until it was certain that no normal rations would arrive. Correctly, 'emergency ration'*

IWT: *Inland Water Transport. The British Army regularly used the canals of France and Belgium to transport supplies*

Jack Johnson: *type of German shell that burst with loud report and black smoke, named after the Negro champion boxer. Some soldiers said that both man and shell had more puff than push*

Jacks, the: *hateful term for military police, especially among Australians*

jagstaffeln: *German fighter flight*

jager: *German rifleman (from* jager – to hunt*)*

jankers: *minor punishment such as being confined to barracks or being required to do fatigue duty*

jasta: *abbreviation for jagstaffeln*

Jerry: *a German, but also applied to any German equipment, such as a Jerry rifle*

jump-off: *to begin an attack*

JUO: *Jam of Uncertain Origin*

kamerad: *(1) literally, comrade or mate; (2) the cry of 'Kamerad!' by Germans wanting to surrender; (3) in British use, the act of kamerading*

KIA: *Killed In Action*

kilo: *abbreviation for kilometre, not kilogram as in modern usage*

Kitch: *Australian and New Zealand nickname for British soldier, supposedly from Kitchener*

Kitchener's Army: *the volunteers raised by Kitchener for the New Armies*

kite balloon: *observation balloon: so called because it was controlled by a cable*

kiwi: *term for a New Zealand soldier. Secondary use: Kiwi brand shoe polish gave its name to RFC and RAF* groundcrew who were noted for their shiny, immaculate appearance

knife rest: *the X-shaped wooden, portable frame covered in barbed wire and used to block trenches or openings in British wire*

kokky-olly birds: *nickname for King's Own Scottish Borderers; KOSB or the 'Kosbies'*

KOYLI: *King's Own Yorkshire Light Infantry*

KR: *King's Regulations. This was an official handbook of rules and regulations*

KSLI: *King's Shropshire Light Infantry*

kultur: *ironic term for German 'frightfulness' – destruction and barbarity (according to Allied propaganda)*

LAB: *Light Armoured Battery – an armoured car*

latrine: *the military WC was dug at the end of a short sap, mostly to the rear of the front, support or reserve trenches. Each company had two 'sanitary personnel' – 'shit wallahs' to the troops – whose duty was to dispose of urine and excreta*

leap-frog: *in this method of assault the first wave took the primary objective, while the second wave leap-frogged to capture the second*

LOB: *Left Out of Battle; the cadre (q.v.) left behind to form the nucleus for rebuilding a unit shattered by battle*

lifebuoy: *nickname for Wex flame-throwers (from the lozenge shape)*

lifting barrage: *gunfire that advanced as the range increased according to a predetermined timetable*

light duty: *army work allotted to a soldier unfit for normal duties, in the trenches or out of them*

line: *usually the front line or firing line. However, 'up the line' meant movement towards the line while 'down the line' indicated movement away from it*

L of C: *Line of Communications. L of C troops belonged to units performing non-battle line functions such as ordnance and supply duties*

listening post: *a dangerously advanced post, often in no-man's-land, where two or three soldiers listened at night for enemy movement*

Long Tom: *long-barrel German long-range gun*

LP: *more commonly L-Pip; Listening Post*

Lucas lamp: *electric-battery signalling lamp*

Maconochie: *canned stew, from the maker's name and unloved by the troops. MM was said to indicate a Maconochie Medal – for eating the stuff. Nonconformist chaplains were also called Maconochies, because 'they were made up of all the leftovers'*

M and V: *canned meat and vegetable ration*

MC: *Military Cross; the junior award to officers*

MD: *Medicine and Duty: The MO's official designation for medicine and duty. It was frequently prescribed for* minor illnesses and often for influenza, bronchitis and serious illnesses when the need for manpower was great. Then even ill men had to stay in the line

medal: *a medal is given for service, or as soldiers would say, 'for having been there'. The only medals given to soldiers who served on the Western Front were the 1914 Star or the 1914–15 Star, the War Medal and the Victory Medal. The great majority of soldiers had only the last two. The army should have awarded 'combat clasps', as in many other British wars, to acknowledge involvement in, say, Loos 1915, Somme 1916 and Hindenburg Line 1917–18. A service medal is not a decoration (q.v.)*

MG: *Machine Gun*

MGC: *Machine-Gun Corps*

Mick: *An Irishman or member of an Irish regiment*

minenwerfer: German trench mortar

minnie: *term for* minenwerfer. *Also Moaning Minnie (from the sound of a bomb in flight)*

mitrailleuse: *French term for machine gun*

MO: *Medical Officer; usually one on the staff of a front unit. A doctor in a base hospital was more likely to be referred to as 'the Doc'*

Moir: *prefab concrete pillbox on the British front in 1918 (from the name of its designer, Sir Ernest Moir). Before 1918 the British had no pillboxes*

mop up: *when infantry moved through enemy trenches some soldiers were left*

to mop up any enemy troops still in dugouts or trenches

mörser: *'mortar' in German. To the British, these particular mortars were heavy howitzers rather than trench mortars*

MT: *Motor Transport*

napoo: *finished, gone, dead; from the French n'y en a plus – 'there's no more'*

no-man's-land: *the ground between the two front lines. Technically, it included the ground covered by the barbed wire of both sides. No-man's-land could be from 10 yd wide to a mile or more*

Number Nine: *the British Army's laxative pill, which was actually stamped 'No. 9'. Many battalion MOs prescribed a course of No. 9s for soldiers they suspected of malingering*

NYD: *Not Yet Diagnosed; the medical term written on labels attached to some casualties. Soldiers quickly gave NYD the meanings of Not Yet Dead, No You Don't and Not Yet Discovered*

NZMR: *New Zealand Mounted Rifles*

NZRB: *New Zealand Rifle Brigade*

OC: *Officer Commanding. In infantry practice this meant the officer in charge of a company, whereas the officer in charge of a battalion was the CO*

odds and sods: *unit personnel, perhaps attached to HQ and not to a company; more frequently odds and sods applied to soldiers not expected to man the parapet, i.e. the cooks and clerks*

oilcan: *German mortar bomb (from the shape)*

old soldier: *not necessarily old by years but by much experience, and generally a wily individual who knew how to 'play the old soldier'*

old and bold: *experienced men, probably with many crimes in their paybook*

old pot and pan: *rhyming slang for the Old Man – the CO*

old sweat: *experienced soldier but without implications of incorrigibility*

orderly: *soldiers detailed for special duty, usually two per platoon each day; the Orderly Officer and Orderly Sergeant were those with many responsibilities and much authority for 24 hours. A medical attendant in a military hospital was also an orderly*

original: *survivor from the initial strength of a unit; a proud label*

over the top: *to go over the parapet in an attack*

O/Rs: *Other Ranks (distinct from officers)*

padre: *military chaplain (from the Spanish for 'priest')*

pals: *battalions of Kitchener's Army raised from a specific locality, such as Burnley Pals, Leeds Pals. The idea was to attract volunteers by promising that they would serve together with their pals*

Panzer: *German tank (from* sturm-panzerkraftwagen*)*

parados: *the rear side of the trench*

parapet: *the side of the trench facing the enemy*

pavé: *stone roads of northern France and Belgium on which many soldiers twisted their ankles and generally ruined their feet*

PBI: *Poor Bloody Infantry*

PC: *French command post;* Poste de Command

perisher: *soldier's term for trench periscope*

P helmet: *phenol helmet, the early gas mask. It was succeeded by the PH helmet, the 'improved' PHG helmet and then the box respirator*

phutt: *to stop functioning or to cease; a trench pump might 'go phutt'*

phonetic alphabet: *soldiers were trained in the phonetic alphabet to avoid confusion in telephone messages. A = ack; B = beer; D = don; P = pip; S = esses; T = toc; and so on*

pickelhaube: *German spiked helmet*

picket: *(1) barbed wire supporting-stake; (2) patrol or sentry*

piggy-stick: *entrenching tool staff (from the bat in some ball games)*

pillbox: *concrete post to protect crew of an MG*

pinard: *French for* vin *– wine*

pineapple: *German grenade (from the shape)*

pip: *officer's star of rank. In Australian trench slang a 'one-pip artist' was a second lieutenant*

Pip, Squeak and Wilfred: *1914 or 1914–15 Star, War and Victory medals (from cartoon characters)*

platoon: *part of an infantry company; usually 30+ men*

plonk: *white wine, from* vin blanc

plug: *a wad of tobacco*

plum and apple: *jam issued to British troops; at first made of these two fruits, then any jam*

PM: *Provost Marshal*

poilu: *French idiom for an infantryman (originally from 'hairy one')*

point blank: *minimum range when using any weapon, from a pistol to an artillery piece*

pom fritz: *British for the French* pommes de terre/frites

pom-pom: *small-calibre cannon (from the drum-like noise)*

poodle-faker: *derisory term for a soldier; generally an officer more concerned with social activity than military duty*

pork and beans: *insulting nickname for Portuguese troops, who were not highly regarded for their military prowess*

portee: *guns carried on trucks*

possie: *Australian for 'position' and much used among diggers; 'This possie will do me!'*

potato-masher: *German stick-grenade (from the shape, with its handle)*

pozzy: *jam*

PPCLI: *Princess Pat's Canadian Light Infantry*

provo: *military policeman; generally a sergeant*

PT: *Physical Training; commonly 'physical jerks'*

PTI: *Physical Training Instructor*

pukka: *genuine or real (from Hindustani)*

pugaree: *the band or cord around a hat,* as with the felt strip worn by Australians and New Zealanders. Also pakri

push: *an attack in great strength, even an offensive. The troops talked of the 'Big Push' when referring to the Battle of the Somme, July 1916*

pusher: *aircraft with rear-mounted propeller*

puttee: *long strip of 4 in cloth rolled around the leg from below the knee to the ankle, forming a gaiter. Puttees were one of the banes of the soldier's life because they were difficult to roll to satisfy an inspecting officer or NCO and they were tight when wet.*

Q: *quartermaster branch*

QF: *Quick-Firer; a gun that did not have to be relaid after each shot because it had hydraulic recoil*

QM: *Quartermaster. In the AIF, the Quarterbloke*

QMG: *Quartermaster General*

RAC: *Royal Air Corps*

RAF: *Royal Air Force, after April 1918*

ragtime: *unsoldierly and inefficient*

Rainbow Division: *US 42nd Division (from its insignia)*

RAMC: *Royal Army Medical Corps. The troops managed to fit malicious/ facetious comments to these capital letters, such as Rob All My Comrades and Rats After Mouldy Cheese*

RAP: *Regimental Aid Post; the busiest place on the battlefield during a battle because nearly all the wounded were first brought here*

racquet-grenade: *explosives fastened to a*

racquet-like handle for achieving greater distance when thown

rataplan: *according to the troops, the sound of machine-gun fire*

RB: *Rifle Brigade*

RDF: *Royal Dublin Fusiliers*

RE: *Royal Engineers*

reading your shirt: *searching for lice (originally Australian)*

red cap: *military police (from the red cover on their caps)*

redoubt: *strongpoint in the trench system*

red triangle men: *YMCA official from his YMCA badge*

register, to: *trial shots when ranging artillery on target – 'One fore, one aft, the next one up his arse'*

respirator: *the more developed gas mask, air being inhaled through chemicals in a metal container*

revally: *phonetic spelling of the reveille bugle call*

revetment: *the strengthening along a trench wall with timber, wire and other substances*

RFA: *Royal Field Artillery*

RFC: *Royal Flying Corps*

RGA: *Royal Garrison Artillery*

RLA: *relay dressing station, for redressing wounds on the way to the rear*

RMA: *Royal Marine Artillery*

RMLI: *Royal Marine Light Infantry*

RMO: *Regimental Medical Officer; the MO in command of the RAP (q.v.)*

RNAS: *Royal Naval Air Service*

RND: *Royal Naval Division*

rocade: *light trench railway. Many rocades ran parallel to the front*

rondins: *logs used to make a corduroy road*

rooti: *bread (from the Hindustani)*

rooty gong: *an award considered trivial because of the belief that it 'came up' with the bread ration*

rosalie: *French nickname for the bayonet*

RSM: *Regimental Sergeant-Major, the most powerful man in the battalion after the CO*

RTO: *Railway Transport Officer, one of whom had an office at every railway station in France used by British and Empire troops*

RTU: *Return To Unit; marked on the papers of all soldiers of any rank who 'failed' on a course*

rum jar: *British term for German mortar bomb (from its shape)*

runner: *soldier carrying messages, in action or in the unit lines*

Russian sap: *narrow trench dug like a horizontal tunnel to avoid disturbing the surface of the ground; raiders could then approach the enemy undetected*

SAA: *Small Arms Ammunition; .303 rounds*

salient: *any trench system protruding into the enemy defensive system. The British position at Ypres was always known as 'The Salient'. Salients were dangerous places because the enemy could fire into them from three directions*

Sallies/salvos: *officers of the Salvation Army who operated tea stalls and rest huts close to the rear lines*

Sammy: *nickname for the American soldier*

sandbag: *sack filled with earth. Trench defences were built from sandbags, largely because sandbags absorbed bullets rather than allowing them to pass through*

san fairy ann: *common British expression expressing total resignation (from ça ne fait rien – it doesn't matter)*

sangar: *rough wall built as a defence against small-arms fire*

sap: *narrow trench, usually for penetration into no-man's-land, dug at an angle to the main trench*

sapper: *the Royal Engineers' private soldier*

sausage: *barrage balloon*

SB: *Stretcher Bearer, identified by his SB or Red Cross brassard*

scran: *food, carried in a scranbag*

shell dressing: *a wound dressing that was larger than a field dressing and included an iodine phial*

shell shock: *medical disorder caused by lengthy or intense exposure to combat and exhaustion. The term came from the belief, in 1915, that shell blasts themselves caused the shock. They contributed to shell shock and no doubt sometimes caused it*

shrapnel: *the steel or lead balls expelled from a certain type of shell in flight. Many soldiers wrongly gave the name shrapnel to shell splinters or shards*

signalese: *the phonetic alphabet*

Silent Percy: *nickname for any gun firing at such long range that it could not be heard. Silent Susan was, for some soldiers, a high-velocity shell*

SIW: *Self-Inflicted Wound. Some soldiers shot themselves in a desperate attempt to escape from the strain of battle and front-line service*

skilly: *watery stew or gruel*

skite: *noun and verb; diggers' slang for a man putting on airs, a boaster*

slack: *debris thrown up by the explosion of a shell or mine; also known as spoil*

SM: *company sergeant-major; correctly the CSM*

SMLE: *Short Magazine Lee-Enfield; the British service rifle*

snob: *a soldier employed on repairing boots*

Soldier's Friend: *a brand of boot polish*

SOS: *combination of coloured rockets fired from the front line or from no-man's-land to request supporting fire*

SPAD: *French aircraft manufacturer and type of plane (from Société Provisoire des Aeroplanes Depardussin)*

splash: *pieces of bullets and shells which penetrated a tank's observation slit*

spout, up the: *invariably used to describe a round in the breach of the rifle*

SRD: *the label on issue rum jars, meaning Service Rum Dilute. The troops had various meanings: Special Rations Department, Seldom Reaches Destination, Soon Runs Dry*

SS: *French field ambulance*

stand-down: *the order to end the stand-to, thus leaving only sentries on guard in trenches*

stand-to: *the order and action of fully*

manning the front trenches at dawn and dusk – and at other times – to repel any attack that might take place

start line: *the white-tape line marking the jumping-off place*

Stellenbosch: *for an officer to be relieved of his command and sent home (from a place-name in the Boer War)*

stick-bomb: *German hand grenade on a handle; the potato-masher (q.v.)*

stinker: *goat-skin jerkin worn over the uniform; it had a rich smell*

stinks: *any soldier working with poison gas*

stosstruppen: *German storm troops; a force much used in 1918*

strafe: *a hail of fire or bombardment; also, to be reprimanded severely*

Stranbaus horn: *an alarm device, generally for gas*

stunt: *freely used to describe any attack, raid or action. The Australians used the term so liberally that it could even mean doing something on leave*

sturmpanzerkraftwagen: *German for 'tank', though abbreviated to panzer*

sturmtruppen: *German storm troops*

suicide club: *bombing party*

swaddy, squaddy: *British private soldier (from an early word for 'bumpkin')*

Système D: *French idiom for muddle (from the verb* se debrouiller *– 'to manage')*

tank: *the code-name for the armoured tractor-like creation which the British first used on the battlefield on 15 September 1916. It was hoped that if the Germans heard of the 'tank' they would expect it to be carrying water*

tankschreken: *meaning 'tank fear', to describe the collapse of morale when the Germans first faced Allied tanks*

tapes: *lines of white tape, usually run out by the unit intelligence officer and his men, to show the start line for an attack and to indicate the direction it should take*

taube: *German for 'dove', the name given to any monoplane but especially to aircraft officially known as Taubes*

teddy bear: *the goat-skin jerkin issued to the British Army in the winter of 1914–15 (from its shaggy appearance)*

terps: *an army interpreter*

terrier: *member of British Territorial Army*

three blue lights: *there was a story that three blue lights would signal the coming of peace. Since peace never seemed to be near, 'three blue lights' came to be a cynical response to anything unbelievable*

Tickler's jam: *a trench-made grenade or bomb, from a common brand of jam. This jam was so common that all jam was called Tickler's*

tictac: *a signaller*

tin hat: *British term for the Breguet aircraft of 1914 (from its metal fuselage when most aircraft were made of wood and canvas). The steel helmet was also known as a tin hat.*

TM: *Trench Mortar*

TMB: *Trench Mortar Battery*

toc emma: *phonetic for TM – Trench Mortar*

Toc H: *the soldiers' club founded by Padre P.B. (Tubby) Clayton following* *a suggestion by Colonel Neville Talbot. Called Talbot House after Lieutenant Gilbert Talbot of the Rifle Brigade, killed in action, it was established in Poperinge, Belgium. It was available to all ranks for rest, recreation and prayer. Known as Toc H from the phonetic alphabet*

toffee apple: *large spherical German mortar bomb with firing shaft attached. Resembling a gigantic toffee apple, it often failed to explode*

Tommy: *the British soldier, the diminutive of Thomas Atkins, the 'standard' name given to the ordinary soldier by the Duke of Wellington. Much used on the Western Front by everybody except the Tommies*

tommy-bar: *spanner for unscrewing the base plug of Mills grenades for insertion of the fuse*

tommy-cooker: *portable stove using solidified alcohol fuel*

torpedo boom: *long wooden pole used to get a tank unditched*

tot: *the rum issue; ⅛ of a pint or ½ gill*

tour of duty: *a unit's period of front-line service*

town major: *the officer responsible for billeting arrangements in a town and for general discipline and organization. He was often a captain, but a major only in a large town*

tracer: *phosphorescent machine-gun bullet which glowed in flight. Since one tracer was used for every seven ordinary rounds it gave a clear indication of the aim*

tractor aircraft: *those with a propeller in front which pulled them along*

trenchée de départ: *French front-line trench*

traverse: *angle in a trench that limited the effect of enfilade fire or shell-burst*

traverser mat: *mat of metal mesh thrown over barbed wire entanglements to allow troops to cross*

trench coat: *belted short overcoat, usually waterproof, worn by officers*

trench foot: *infection of the foot, from standing in water and mud. It often caused gangrene, leading to amputation*

tromblon: *French cup-shaped discharger for firing a grenade from a rifle*

trooper: *cavalry private; also a troop-ship*

Uhlan: *German lancer, much feared in 1914–15*

Uncle Charlie: *full marching order*

unteroffizier: *German corporal. In the German Army an* unteroffizier *had the authority of a British sergeant*

VAD: *Voluntary Aid Detachment and the name for the individual nurses*

valise: *an officer's bedroll and equipment, though knapsacks were sometimes known as valises*

VB: *the French Vivien Bessières rifle grenade*

vermorel sprayer: *a device with a chemical to disperse low-lying gas*

Very: *the ubiquitous signal or illuminating flare, fired from a Very pistol, named after the inventor S.W. Very*

WAAC: *Women's Auxillary Army Corps*

wad: *a bun*

waler: *breed of Australian horse; the mount of the Australian Light Horse*

walking wounded: *men wounded but, with wounds dressed, able to walk to the rear for further attention*

wallah: *the name added to a soldier's function, such as transport wallah, intelligence wallah, armourer wallah*

Whippet: *a particular light tank and then, from usage, any light tank*

Whistling William: *an enemy shell that emitted a whistling noise*

white star: *chlorine and phosgene gas in combination; a deadly mixture*

whizzbang: *a high-velocity, low-trajectory shell that made a shrill approach noise and then a sharp explosive report*

WIA: *Wounded In Action*

Wipers: *British and Empire troops' affectionate name for Ypres*

WO: *Warrant Officer and War Office, though among officers the War Office was more generally known as the War House*

Woodbine: *popular and plentiful cheap cigarette; also an Australian name for British troops in 1916*

wooden track: *another name for a corduroy road (q.v.)*

woolly bear: *the black cloud of smoke from the burst of a type of German shell*

wristwatch: *classy because wristwatches were fashionable at the time; it was said, for instance, that a certain officer had 'wristwatch' style*

'Y', the: *the YMCA*

yellow cross: *mustard gas (from the symbol painted on the shells)*

YMCA: *Young Men's Christian Association, which ran rest huts and canteens close to the front. 'Y Emma' to the British, 'the Y' to Americans and Australians*

Yperite: *French name for mustard gas but common in all armies*

'Z': *for Zero hour, the time that an attack commenced*

Zepp: *general abbreviation for a German Zeppelin*

MAPS OF THE WESTERN FRONT

The Western Front 1914–18.

73

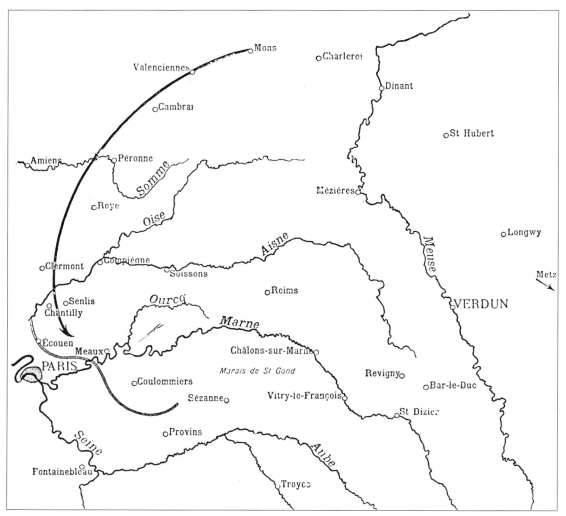

The Battle of the Marne, 1914.

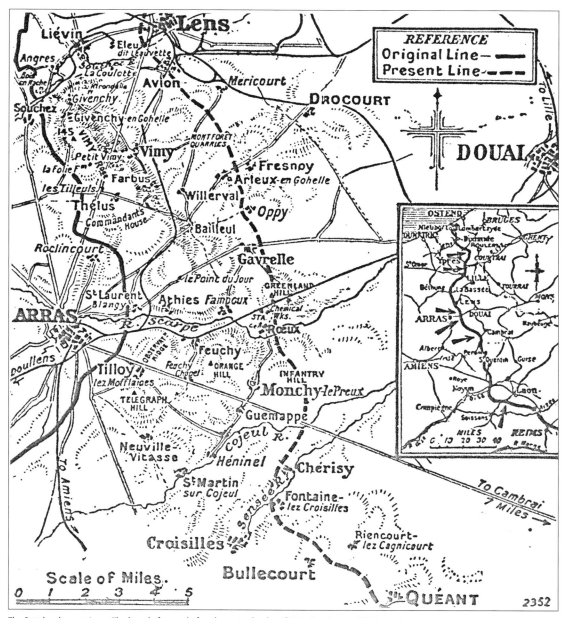

The British salient at Arras. The lines before and after the spring battles of 9 April to 5 June 1917 are shown.

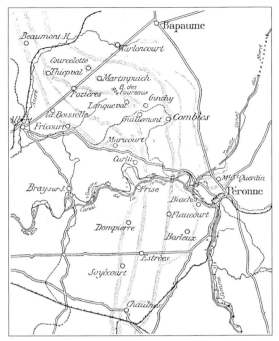

The German lines of resistance (dotted) in the Battle of the Somme, 1916.

The front line from June 1915 to June 1917.

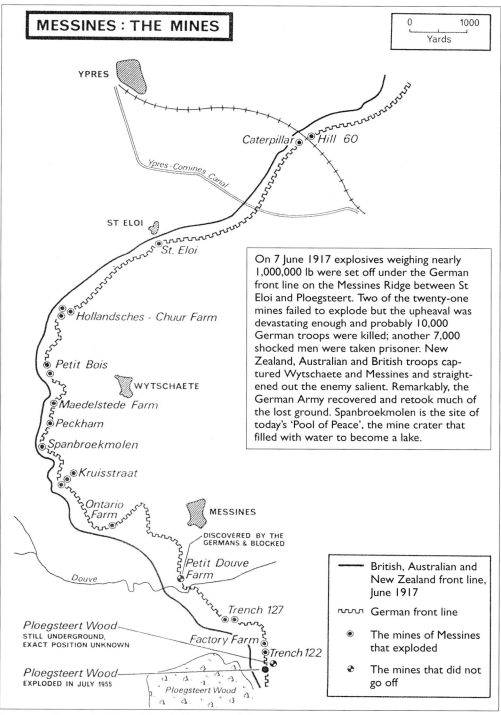

MESSINES : THE MINES

0   1000
Yards

YPRES

Caterpillar ⊙ ● *Hill 60*

Ypres-Comines Canal

ST ELOI

⊙ *St. Eloi*

⊙⊙ *Hollandsches - Chuur Farm*

⊙ *Petit Bois*
⊙

WYTSCHAETE

⊙ *Maedelstede Farm*

⊙ *Peckham*

⊙ *Spanbroekmolen*

⊙ *Kruisstraat*
⊙⊙

Ontario Farm

MESSINES

DISCOVERED BY THE
GERMANS & BLOCKED

Petit Douve Farm

Douve

Trench 127
⊙⊙

Ploegsteert Wood
STILL UNDERGROUND,
EXACT POSITION UNKNOWN

Factory Farm

Trench 122

Ploegsteert Wood
EXPLODED IN JULY 1955

Ploegsteert Wood

On 7 June 1917 explosives weighing nearly 1,000,000 lb were set off under the German front line on the Messines Ridge between St Eloi and Ploegsteert. Two of the twenty-one mines failed to explode but the upheaval was devastating enough and probably 10,000 German troops were killed; another 7,000 shocked men were taken prisoner. New Zealand, Australian and British troops captured Wytschaete and Messines and straightened out the enemy salient. Remarkably, the German Army recovered and retook much of the lost ground. Spanbroekmolen is the site of today's 'Pool of Peace', the mine crater that filled with water to become a lake.

——— British, Australian and New Zealand front line, June 1917

ᴧᴧᴧᴧ German front line

⊙ The mines of Messines that exploded

◐ The mines that did not go off

The mines at Messines, from Martin Gilbert's highly recommended *First World War Atlas*.

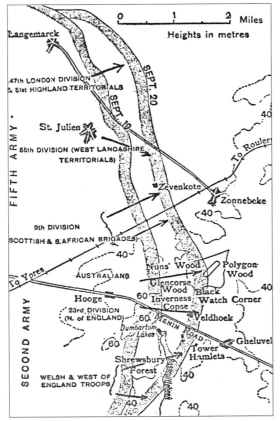

Map showing the British advance in the battle of 20 September 1917.

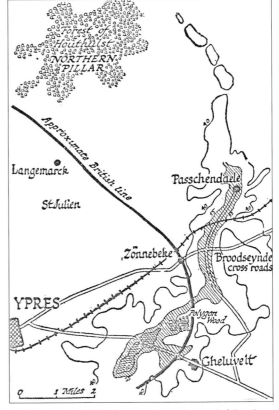

The 26 September 1917 advance on the southern end of the ridges, resulting in the capture of Polygon Wood.

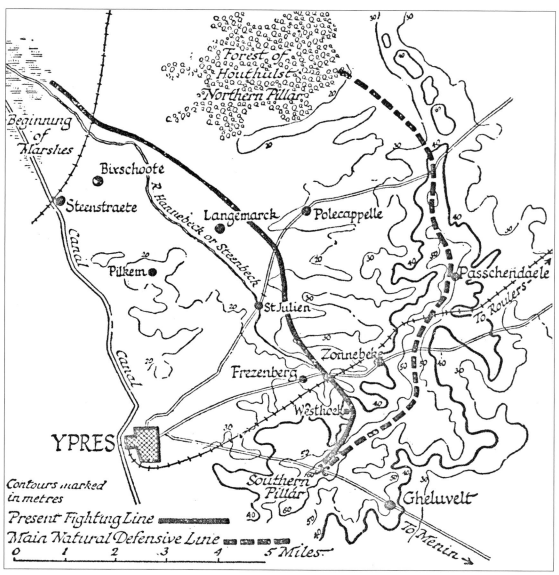

This map, from *Land & Water*, shows the crest of ridges (broken line) and advance (solid line) in the third battle beyond Langemarck in October 1917. The southern pivot or pillar is at X; note also 'Clapham Junction' (Hill 60), 1 mile south of the Menin Road.

Allied ground lost in the First (21–8 March) and Second (9–18 April) phases of the German Spring Offensive in 1918.

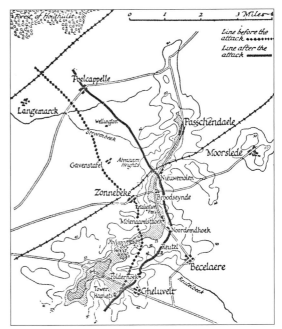

The extent of the ground gained in the British attack of 4 October 1917 (solid line). Poelcappelle was soon retaken by the enemy in a counter-attack. The 55 m contour is shaded.

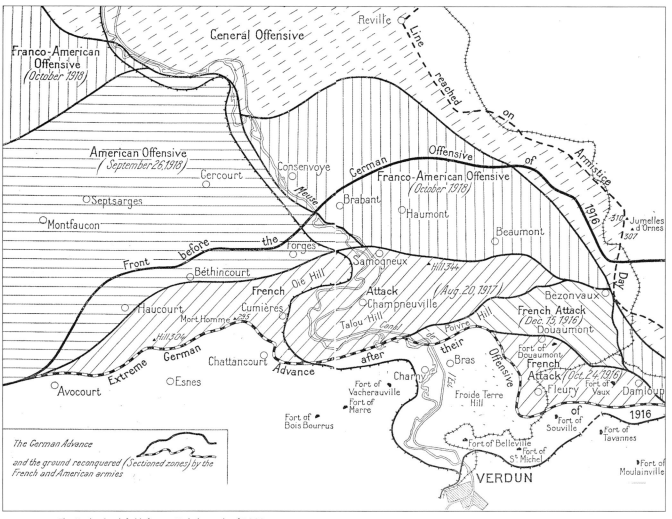

The Verdun battlefield, from a Michelin guide of 1920.

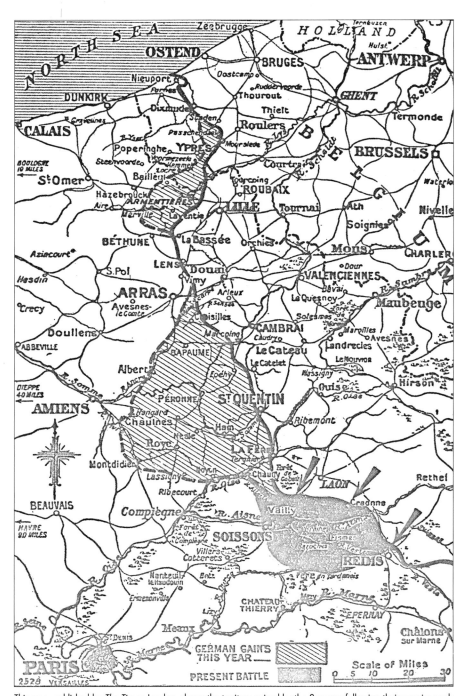

This map, published by *The Times*, London, shows the territory gained by the Germans following their massive push in March 1918. The black region is the 'Great Tardenois Bulge', Third Phase, on 31 May 1918. The advance was about to run out of steam.

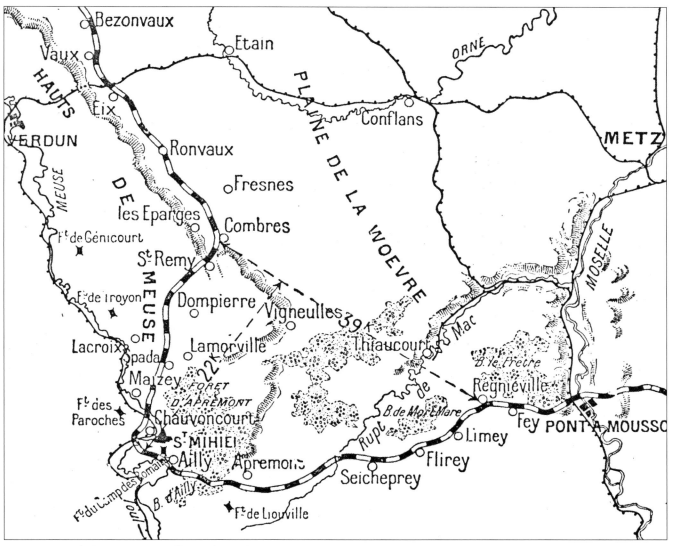

St Mihiel Salient prior to the offensive of September 1918.

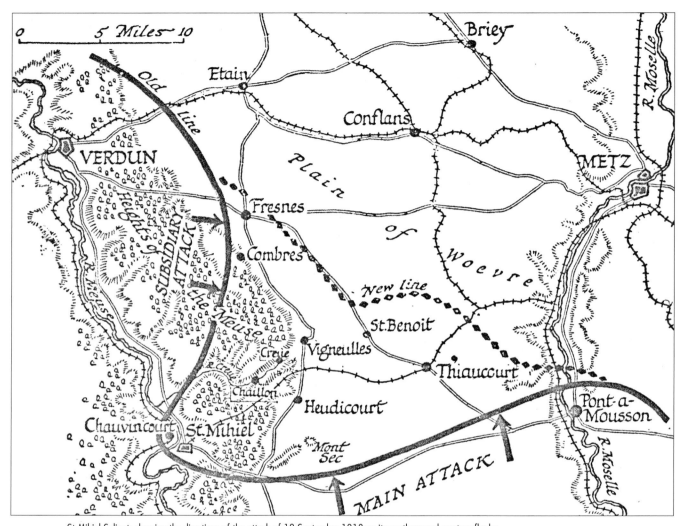

St Mihiel Salient, showing the directions of the attack of 12 September 1918 on its southern and western flanks.

This contemporary map shows the counter-attacks of 7 June 1918 against the new German salient by the French west of Soissons, the Americans west of Château-Thierry, and the British south-west of Rheims.

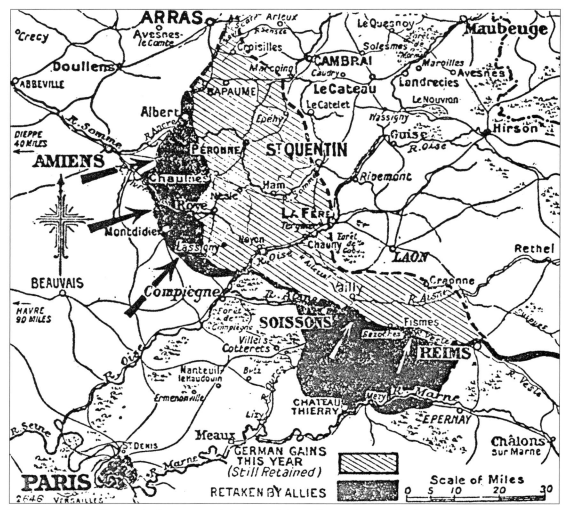

The new Anglo-French offensive in the Amiens sector, which began on 8 August. The ground recovered by the Allies from 18 July to 11 August 1918 is shown in black.

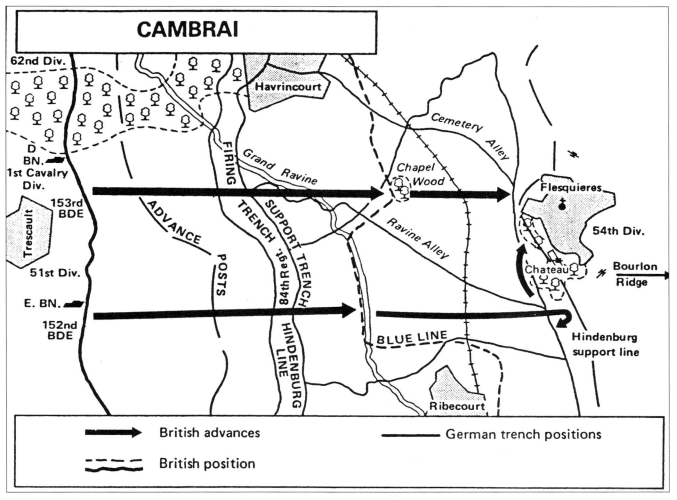

Cambrai, November 1917: the Great British Tank Attack.

The German thrust towards Compiègne, the abortive Fourth Phase of 1918, was an attempt to straighten the German front from the Oise to the Marne.

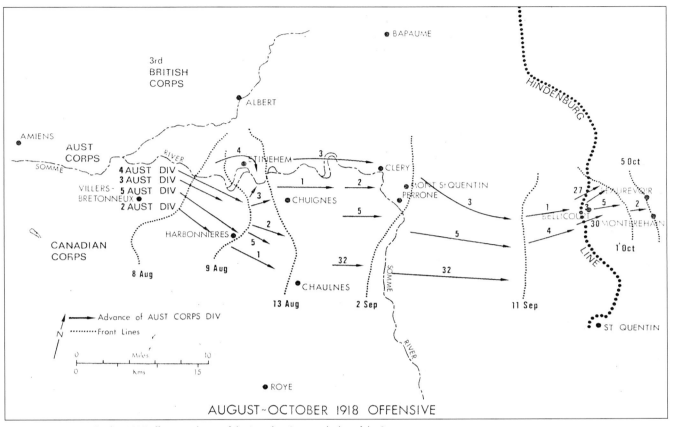

AUGUST~OCTOBER 1918 OFFENSIVE

August–October 1918 offensive: advance of the Australian Corps on the line of the Somme.

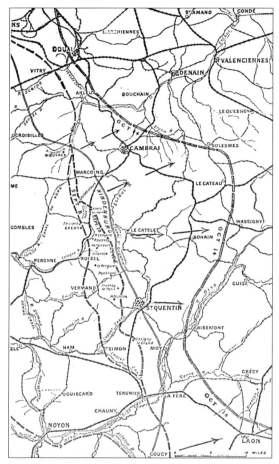

Map showing the breaking of the Hindenburg Line and the capture by the British of Le Cateau, La Fére and Laon in October 1918.

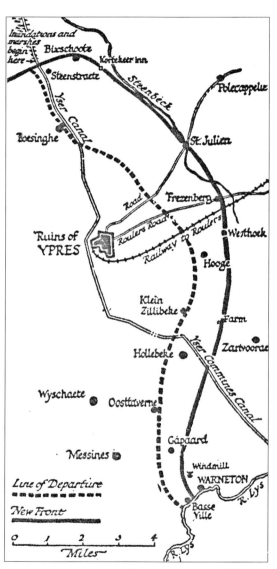

The advance in the First Battle, 1918: the French on the left have reached Steenbeck; the Fifth Army is in the centre; the Second Army with the Australians and New Zealanders is on the right opposite Messines. St Julien and Westhoek were lost soon afterwards in counter-attacks.

CHAPTER FIVE

OFFENSIVES, BATTLES, CAMPAIGNS

An offensive was the largest form of hostile movement against the enemy. It should not be confused with a 'general advance' since this did not necessarily involve actual fighting. The offensive was larger in scale and in the number of men involved than a battle, though this term is now an amorphous one. The dimensions of an offensive might be expressed as follows: the Somme Offensive was made up of many battles, including the Battle of Pozières, and the battles of Flers, Delville Wood, Mametz, Grandcourt, Beaumont-Hamel and so on. Following the German withdrawal (not a retreat) from the Somme and elsewhere, there was a general Allied advance. The great British offensive in the Ypres Salient in the latter part of 1917 was similarly made up of many battles.

Planning for an offensive required great effort by all arms and especially for the artillery. On the Western Front a scale of one gun every 30 yd was 'normal'; that is, when conditions on the front were static. A projected offensive meant that one gun was required for every 10 yd of the length of front affected. This does not mean that the guns were lined up as far as the eye could see with the guns in a straight line. A balance had to be struck with the deployment of field guns, medium guns and heavy guns. The French had an almost rigid mathematical formula for the use of guns during an offensive. It called for one field gun every 15 yd, one medium or heavy gun for the destruction of the enemy lines each 30 yd, and a 'superheavy' gun every 150–200 yd. In addition, there was what the French called 'trench artillery' – the mortars, with a frequency of one every 30 yd.

In March 1918, when the Germans launched their remarkable attempts at breakthrough, they used a weight of guns so massive that the mere statistics would have caused alarm on some parts of the Allied front. On a 50 mile front, the German High Command called up the following guns for each mile: 92 field guns, 31 field howitzers, 14 medium howitzers, 14 heavy guns, 7 heavy howitzers and 4 superheavy howitzers. Further to increase the weight of metal exploding on the British and French defenders, the Germans shelled alternate stretches of the Allied lines, so that each

Heavy artillery moves up in 1918. (From a painting by Georges Scott)

stretch was pounded with double the normal number of guns; for instance, 184 field guns to the mile. This was an offensive with a vengeance.

British artillery could also put down a barrage of terrifying intensity. To soften up the Messines sector in preparation for the British–Australian–New Zealand attack on 6 June 1917, the artillery began its pounding of the German lines on 26 May. It fired 3.5 million shells before the first Allied infantryman left his trench for the assault.

At that time most generals of all armies believed that a prolonged bombardment was essential for an infantry attack to succeed. The truth was that heavy bombardment often worked against the attackers because it warned the enemy of an impending attack and broke up the ground so badly, or caused such bogs and mire to develop, that advancing soldiers lost cohesion and direction. The bombardment often fell abortively. The Germans did not remain in the one place

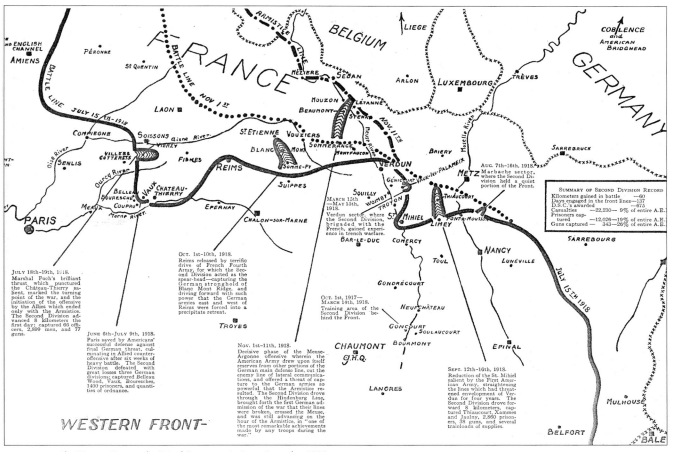

The Western Front as the United States saw it, June–November 1918.

to be pounded to pieces by several days' shelling; they quickly moved to alternative, emergency positions.

If, on the Western Front, most battles took place as part of an offensive, a campaign was a more general term embracing a series of actions, large and small. In Western Front terms it usually referred to a geographical area, a topographical region or a period. Official histories, for instance, refer to

the Artois campaign of 1915–16 or to 'the Australians' final campaign of the war', meaning the series of battles and actions between 8 August and 5 October 1918.

The offensives, battles and campaigns that follow make up a considerable part of the war on the Western Front but to cover all the encounters that might be termed 'battles' would require a large volume devoted exclusively to them.

AISNE RIVER: 1914, 1917, 1918

The Battle of the Aisne covers a number of actions in the vicinity of the Aisne river, northern France.

Aisne I: The August 1914 battle was a prelude to the more important Battle of the Marne. The French, under pressure from the Germans, retired on 29 August behind the protection of the Aisne river.

Aisne II: Following the Battle of the Marne, the German Army also crossed the Aisne on 13 September. The French and British pursued and a stand-off battle was fought until 18 September.

Aisne III: On 6 April 1917 a new Aisne battle commenced and by the 16th was fully in gear when General Nivelle, the new commander-in-chief, launched an offensive on the 50 mile front between Soissons and Reims. The French claimed nearly 30,000 prisoners but they too suffered heavily and their offensive died on 9 May. On 15 May General Pétain succeeded Nivelle and was faced with open mutiny among the demoralized French troops.

Aisne IV: Part of Ludendorff's third offensive of 1918. The Germans struck at the French Sixth Army in the Chemin-des-Dames area and, with forty-one divisions and a sustained artillery barrage from 4,600 guns, overwhelmed the French. On 27 May they pushed a 13 mile bulge in the French lines, the greatest one-day advance anywhere in four years. On 30 May the Germans reached the Marne and the offensive ceased on 6 June. During this enemy offensive the Americans regained Belleau Wood and won their first victory of the war at Cantigny.

ALBERT: 1914 AND 1918

A key position on the Western Front, Albert gave its name to a series of complex actions, many of them fought at a distance from the town. The only real battle of Albert itself took place on 25–9 September 1914, when the French held the town against a German attack. The final Allied assault of August 1918 used Albert as a major starting point.

AMIENS: 8 AUGUST–3 SEPTEMBER 1918

This battle, between 8 August and 3 September 1918, was the second Allied offensive of 1918. The plan was to reduce the enemy salient pointing at the city of Amiens, from which the Germans could shell the Paris–Amiens railway. The main assault was delivered by General Rawlinson's Fourth Army, with seventeen divisions, including one American, four Canadian and five Australian, the entire Australian force. Advancing on a 10 mile front against twenty German divisions, the Allies took 16,000 prisoners in two hours and penetrated 9 miles by nightfall. The fiercest fighting fell to the Australians at Villers Bretonneux. General Ludendorff called 8 August 'the black day of the German Army'. On 10 August the French Third Army attacked the southern side of the salient and on 21 August the British Third and First armies also attacked. By 3 September the Allies had forced the

Germans back to the Hindenburg Line. The Germans suffered 75,000 casualties, including 30,000 prisoners, the British and Empire forces 22,000 and the French 24,000.

ANTWERP: OCTOBER 1914

In August 1914 the main Belgian army of 150,000 fell back from their front line to a second line at Antwerp, which the Germans needed to hold to protect their rear. On 1 October General von Beselar's heavy siege guns began to smash Antwerp's forts one by one. On 6 October King Albert evacuated his army from the city, linked with the British and finally took up positions on the extreme left of the Western Front. Antwerp's inner forts fell on 8 October and the Germans entered next day to impose a 'levy' of £20 million.

A French soldier wounded during the fighting in the Argonne receives first-aid treatment.

ARGONNE FOREST: 1915–18

For three years, from 5 October 1915 until 3 November 1918, many actions occurred in the Argonne area, which lies between the regions of Champagne and Lorraine. The main battle began on 26 September 1918, when a combined American–French force attacked the Germans on a 40 mile front. The Americans, on the right, advanced 7 miles. More than 1,200,000 Americans were in action at one time or another during the forty-seven days of fighting. Difficulties of supply and communication, and the inexperience of the American troops imposed great strain on the US High Command, under General John Pershing.

On 2 October a battalion of the 77th Division, under Major C.W. Whittlesey, was surrounded and became known as the 'Lost Battalion'. The survivors held out with great courage until they were relieved on the 8th. Between 26 September and 11 November twenty-two American and six French divisions, with an approximate strength of 500,000, engaged forty-three German divisions, totalling 470,000 troops. Casualties: American, 50,000 killed or wounded; German, 100,000, together with 26,000 prisoners. They lost 800 guns and 3,000 machine guns.

ARRAS: 4 APRIL–3 MAY 1917

Fighting was intermittent in the Arras sector and the main battle commenced on 4 April 1917, when the British began a massive artillery bombardment with 2,800 guns on a 20 mile front. On 9 April the Canadian Corps of General Horne's First Army, together with General Allenby's Third Army, commenced the infantry assault. They gained 3½ miles but the German Sixth Army commander, General von Falkenhausen, threw in strong reserves. General Gough's Fifth Army in the southern flank could make no impression on the German lines but the attack was pressed until 3 May to divert enemy attention from the even greater attack along the Aisne. The British and Empire forces suffered 84,000 casualties in the battle, and the Germans 70,000.

ARTOIS: 9 MAY–18 JUNE 1915

Between 9 May and 18 June 1915 the French and Germans fought a senseless battle of attrition on a 6 mile front north of Arras. The Germans were pushed back 3 miles and the French gained some ground on Vimy Ridge. British troops supported the French at Festubert on 26 May but lost heavily. Powerful German counter-attacks threw the French back but a steady slaughter continued until 18 June. The French suffered 100,000 casualties and the Germans 75,000.

AUCHONVILLERS: 26 MARCH 1918

On 26 March 1918 the New Zealand Division was rushed into action to halt a powerful German attack which was threatening to break the Allied lines. Fighting took place at Mailly-Maillet, Hamel and Rossignol Wood. Australian units, on the New Zealanders' left flank, fought at Hébuterne Wood.

BAPAUME: 21 AUGUST–1 SEPTEMBER 1918

Following the German withdrawal from Bapaume in March 1917, Australian units occupied it but no fighting occurred. The Battle of Bapaume took place between 21 August and 1 September 1918, when the New Zealand Division attacked the formidable Le Transloy–Loupert system and captured Grevillers, Avesnes-les-Bapaume, Favreuil and Fremicourt. They took 1,647 prisoners but suffered 1,845 casualties in the process.

BASSEVILLE: JULY 1918

New Zealanders captured this strong German position on 27 July 1917, lost it in a German counterattack and retook it on 31 July. They suffered only 38 casualties to the Germans' 112.

BELLEAU WOOD: 6 JUNE–1 JULY 1918

In an offensive which began on 6 June 1918 the Germans captured Belleau Wood, on the Metz–Paris road, and held it with four divisions. On 6 June the US Second Division, under General Bundy,

Americans in action in Belleau Wood, near Cambrai. This was one of their first significant battles on the Western Front.

was ordered to retake the mile-square forest, a task that occupied the Americans until 1 July and cost them 9,777 casualties, including 1,811 killed. German casualties are unknown but 1,600 were taken prisoner.

BROODSEINDE RIDGE: 4–5 OCTOBER 1917

The most important of the Australians' actions of late 1917 and potentially the most decisive. They were at the centre of a line of twelve divisions, the others being British together with the New Zealand Division on a 10 mile front. In a well-led attack the Australians crossed the Passchendaele–Beselare road, giving them possession of strategic higher ground. Triumphant on a ridge used by the Germans for dominant observation, the Australians came under shellfire. Despite its losses the AIF counted the Battle of Broodseinde one of its great successes.

BULLECOURT I: 10–11 APRIL 1917

The Australian Fourth Division was ordered to capture part of the Hindenburg Line. Without an artillery barrage, failed by tanks and attacking against uncut belts of barbed wire, the Australians took and held part of the Hindenburg Line. This was a remarkable feat but the attackers were left without support and the survivors were forced to withdraw. The division suffered 3,000 casualties, including 28 officers and 1,142 men captured.

BULLECOURT II: 3–26 MAY 1917
This was one of the great battles of the war, though only part of a major British assault on a 20 mile front. Units of three Australian divisions, the First, Second and Fifth, attacked German positions known as OG1 and OG2 Lines with the objective of capturing some villages behind them. The fighting everywhere else died down, so that all attention was focused on the Bullecourt battle. The Australians took and held more than 2 miles of the enemy lines, beating off seven major counterattacks and many minor ones. They suffered 7,000 casualties.

CAMBRAI: 20 NOVEMBER–4 DECEMBER 1917
The first great tank battle in history. Tanks had been useless in the mud of Flanders and the British advocates of tank warfare looked for dry, hard ground. They found it at Cambrai. Haig would allow an attack only when his great offensive in Flanders had stopped, because he had no infantry rein-forcements to spare. The Cambrai Offensive was under the operational control of General Sir Julian Byng, while the new Tank Corps was commanded by Major-General Hugh Elles. A total of 381 tanks went forward in massed formation, without any preliminary bombardment, and took the Germans by surprise. Though the tanks could move at only a walking pace, they punched a 6 mile hole in the lines of the German Second Army, under General von Marwitz. This was a greater success than anything achieved on the Somme or in Flanders, and the cost was cheap for the time – 1,500 British losses against 10,000 German prisoners and 200 guns. In London, church bells were rung for the only time in the war, to celebrate victory. Infantry made the gap into a salient but failure to exploit the advantage, lack of knowledge about infantry–tank cooperation and rapid German defensive action prevented the British from making the most of the initial success. Haig was forced to order a withdrawal on 4 December and all territorial gains were lost. The British suffered 43,000 casualties, including 6,000 prisoners taken on 30 November, the first day of the German counteroffensive. The Germans lost 41,111 men, including 11,000 captured.

CANTIGNY: 28 MAY 1918
On the second day of the great German offensive along the Aisne, the American First Division under General R.E. Bullard captured Cantigny, which was held by elements of the German Eighteenth Army, commanded by General von Hutier. With a loss of 1,607 casualties, the Americans held the position against fierce counter-attacks.

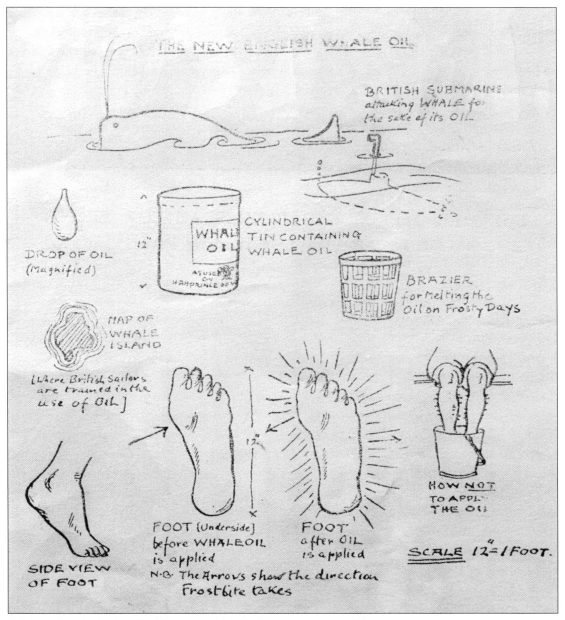

Applications of whale oil to the soldiers' feet were considered the best way to prevent trench foot.

CELTIC WOOD

We know little of the 'battle' that took place here, but as it hardly qualifies for the chapter 'Places to See' I am describing it here. On 8 October 1917 Lieutenant F.J. Scott, Tenth Battalion AIF, led eighty-four officers and men in a raid on German positions in Celtic Wood, Broodseinde Ridge. The party suffered some casualties before the main group entered the wood. Here they disappeared and only fourteen men who had been wounded earlier returned to Australian lines. The Red Cross received no list of prisoners from the Germans and, after the war passed beyond Broodseinde Ridge, graves registration officers found no trace of the Australians. In the 1990s a British researcher, Tony Spagnoly, exhaustively researched the Celtic Wood affair and traced certain names, but thirty-seven Australians remain unaccounted for. The site of Celtic Wood, which was cleared away many years ago, is off Spilstraat, which itself turns off the Passchendaele–Beselare road, near Zonnebeke, Ypres Salient.

CHAMPAGNE CAMPAIGNS

Between 20 December and 17 March 1915 the French Army lost many soldiers in vain attacks – more like suicidal charges – against German machine guns. On 25 September 1915 General Joffre launched another attack under generals Pétain and de Cary, and by 6 November they had captured 25,000 Germans and 150 guns, but at a terrible cost of 145,000 casualties. Both sides held their original positions. Between 15 and 17 July 1918 the Germans went on the offensive in the Champagne sector and crossed the Marne river.

CHEMIN-DES-DAMES

The forested country on either side of this long ridge road in eastern France was the scene of some of the war's most bitter fighting and the arena for several major actions. On 9 September 1914 the French attacked and pushed back the Germans. In 1915–16 the sector was the scene of

Kaiser Wilhelm II, on the right, receives the King of Saxony in June 1918. At that time the Kaiser still believed he could win the war.

constant but indecisive fighting. In April 1917 the ill-fated Nivelle Offensive took place here, with the French losing 120,000 men in five days. On 14 July a great artillery battle raged across Chemin-des-Dames, without gain to either side. On 27 May 1918 the Germans attacked and broke through to the Marne. The Kaiser visited the battlefield in triumph but by 11 October his armies had evacuated it. More than 100,000 men were killed in or around Chemin-des-Dames.

EAUCOURT L'ABBAYE

This village, north-west of Martinpuich, was one of the many British targets for capture during the Battle of the Somme in 1916. The fighting on 1 October was notable in that the first New Zealand VC of the war was won. The recipient was Sergeant Donald Brown of the Otago Regiment, but he was killed in the action. Lieutenant-Colonel R.B.T. Bradford of the Ninth Durham Battalion was awarded the VC for 'his most conspicuous bravery and good leadership' on the same day.

FLANDERS

Flanders is the historic general name given to the battlefield which stretched from the Lys river in northern France to the Yser river in Belgium. The main focus of battle was the large town of Ypres (now Ieper), and the term 'Ypres Salient' is often used to mean all of Flanders. In this lowland killing field many battles took place, mainly between British and Empire troops and the Germans. However, French troops were also involved, while the Belgian Army held the left of the line from Boezinge to Dixmuide and Nieuport. In 1918 two American divisions were engaged in the fighting.

The main places where local battles occurred were: Armentières, Comines, Warneton, Wytschaete, Messines, Zillebeke, Broodseinde, Zonnebeke, Kemmel, Hooge, Pilckem, St Julien, Langemarck, Passchendaele, Poelcapelle, Ploegsteert, Houthulst Forest, Staden, Veldhoek, Gheluveldt, Oostaverne, St Jean and St Eloi. The British gave various names to significant points within Flanders, such as Hill 60, Hill 62, Hill 63, Polygon Wood, Sanctuary Wood, Hellfire Corner, Tower Hamlets, Shrewsbury Forest and many others. The British suffered more than a million casualties in Flanders, including the 150,000 men who died in the fourteen weeks of the Third Battle of Ypres, which is sometimes known as the Battle of Passchendaele. During Fourth Ypres (also known as the Battle of Lys) there were 240,000 British casualties, while the Germans, the attackers on that occasion, had 348,000. During the preliminary bombardment for Third Ypres the British fired 4,283,550 shells, a total of 107,000 tons. These shells destroyed the complex drainage system of Flanders and produced a vast bog. The British attacks gained little ground and even these small gains were lost to the great German offensive of March–April 1918.

Charging infantry – part of a long line of men – clear some barbed wire and head across no-man's-land. The generals kept on ordering attacks such as this, always with only the faintest chance of success, always with heavy casualties.

FORT DOUAUMENT: 25 FEBRUARY 1916
This great and much-battered fort was a key position in the defences of Verdun. Following vicious fighting the Germans captured it but the French retook it on 2 November 1916.

FRONTIERS OF FRANCE: 20–4 AUGUST 1914
The name given to a five-day battle which took place over an area stretching from the Swiss frontier to Mons, Belgium. The Germans committed seven armies, the French five and the British one. The different segments were the battles of Lorraine, Ardennes, Sambre (also known as the Battle of Charleroi) and Mons. The French and their British allies suffered disastrous defeats. Of the 1,250,000 French troops involved, 300,000 became casualties, though the German losses were of similar magnitude. At Mons the British had 4,244 casualties in holding up the German advance for nine hours. The battles established the tactics and strategy – or more correctly the lack of sensible tactics – of the war. The Germans depended on massive frontal attacks supported by drenching artillery and

machine-gun fire. The defenders also used massed guns and machine guns. The overall German commander was Field Marshal von Moltke, under whom were generals von Heeringen, Prince Rupprecht of Bavaria, Crown Prince Friedrich Wilhelm, von Hausen, von Bülow and von Kluck. Under General Joffre, the French commander, were generals Dubail, de Castelnau, de Cary, Ruffey, Foch and Lanrezac. The British generals were Sir John French in command, and Smith-Dorrien.

LE CATEAU: 26 AUGUST 1914

This was the biggest battle fought by the British since Waterloo in 1815. Following the general withdrawal of the British Expeditionary Force on 23 August, the German First Army closely pursued. British II Corps, under Lieutenant-General Smith-Dorrien, cut off from I Corps (Lieutenant-General Douglas Haig), stood and fought at Le Cateau, 36 miles south of Mons, from where the retreat had started. In taking this action, which was generally considered correct and courageous, Smith-Dorrien was disobeying his commander-in-chief, General French. On 16 August his three divisions gave battle to von Kluck's whole First Army and struggled to avoid a double envelopment. After eleven hours Smith-Dorrien disengaged, having enabled the BEF to escape. The British suffered 8,000 casualties, a fifth of their total force, and lost thirty-eight guns, but they inflicted heavy casualties on the

Germans. Smith-Dorrien lost his job as a result of his disobedience.

LIÈGE: 4 AUGUST 1914

The first German attack of the war. Enemy units entered the fortress city on 7 August, but eleven of the twelve forts guarding the city held out until 16 August.

LYS RIVER (OR YPRES IV): 9–17 APRIL 1918

This battle was the key action of Marshal Ludendorff's second offensive of 1918. From Armentières, Ludendorff used General Quast's Sixth Army to strike at the centre of the British First Army under General A. Horne. The Germans overwhelmed a Portuguese division and this resulted in the British line being driven back by 5 miles. Next day General von Arnim's Fourth Army threw back the British Second Army, under General Plumer. Messines Ridge, won by British, Australian and New Zealand troops at great cost in 1917, was lost. On 11 April the German armies linked for a massive drive to the sea. Next day Field Marshal Haig issued his famous 'Backs to the Wall' order, forbidding any further retirement. All available units were rushed into the line, including some French divisions sent by Marshal Foch, the Allied commander-in-chief. The German drive captured a strip of land 10 miles deep but on 17 April it was halted. After further attacks and counter-attacks Ludendorff stopped the operation. He had won a tactical victory but now he held a salient that was difficult to defend, and he had suffered 350,000 casualties. Allied losses were 305,000, nearly all British.

MARNE RIVER I: 6–8 SEPTEMBER 1914
General von Kluck's First Army reached the Marne on 3 September 1914 and crossed it only a day behind the retreating French Fifth Army of General d'Esperey and the BEF led by General French. Von Kluck believed that the Allies were close to defeat and on 5 September, when he reached a point directly east of Paris, he paused for a final thrust. However, General von Moltke, chief of the German general staff, feared that the right of the German advance was exposed and ordered von Kluck to withdraw to the north. This gave the Allied commander-in-chief, General Joffre, a slight respite. On the morning of 6 September French divisions under General Maunory, commander of the Sixth Army, and General Gallieni, military governor of Paris, launched a surprise counteroffensive along the Ourcq river against the German IV Reserve Corps under General Gronau. A 30 mile gap opened up between the German First and Second armies and the British and French armies moved into it. At the same time the French Ninth Army of General Foch attacked at the junction of the German Second and Third armies.

The battle raged along a 300 mile front, with the French barely able to hold their ground. Vital reinforcements brought back from the Moselle front were rushed into action by fleets of Paris taxis. On the eastern end of the French line the First and Second armies clung to the fortress cities of Epinal, Charmes and Nancy along the Moselle. In between the two fronts the French Third and Fourth armies stopped the German drive from the direction of Verdun.

Von Moltke called off the German attack on 9 September and the entire German line began a fighting withdrawal to the line of the Aisne river, 40 miles away. Following this reverse, von Moltke lost his job to von Falkenhayn.

The British Army was the only Allied force which advanced continually through 5–8 September and it was the only army to cross the Marne before the German retreat. This enemy retreat was largely the result of the vigorous British action. With only 70,000 effective troops – following heavy losses at Mons and Le Cateau – the British Army achieved more than could have been expected of it. However, some historians believe that Sir John French could have broken the German lines had he attacked even more resolutely.

The Germans committed forty-four infantry, and seven cavalry divisions, a total of 900,000 men. The Allies used fifty-six infantry and nine cavalry divisions, making an enormous force of 1,082,000 men. French casualties were almost 250,000 and the German about 200,000, but no accurate figures are available. British casualties were 1,071.

MARNE RIVER II (ALSO KNOWN AS CHAMPAGNE–MARNE OFFENSIVE): 15 JULY–6 AUGUST 1918

General Ludendorff launched a major attack by fifty-two divisions on the Allied line and his Seventh Army, under General von Boehn, established a bridgehead 9 miles long and 4 miles deep. The French, with spirited assistance from the Americans' Third Division, checked the enemy advance. Thirty-six Allied divisions were involved in the fighting – twenty-three French, nine American, two British and one Italian. The Champagne–Marne Offensive was the last major German thrust on the Western Front.

On 18 July, Marshal Foch, the Allied commander-in-chief, mounted a massive counterattack with four entire French armies and fourteen Allied divisions, supported by 350 tanks. This powerful thrust threatened to cut German communications along the Soissons–Château Thierry road, forcing Ludendorff to withdraw. He formed a line along the Vesle and Aisne rivers which was strong enough, on 6 August, to beat off an American attack. Allied casualties amounted to 60,000, including 20,000 dead. German casualties were at least 100,000.

MENIN ROAD, FLANDERS: 20–30 SEPTEMBER 1917

The Australian First and Second divisions formed the striking centre of eleven divisions of the British Second and Fifth armies. The Australians suffered 5,013 casualties in the attack, which pushed the Germans back on their defences along the Broodseinde–Passchendaele Ridge.

MESSINES, FLANDERS: 7–14 JUNE 1917

The Germans had contained the British within the Ypres Salient for thirty months. To break out of it, General Haig had first to throw the Germans from Messines Ridge, which commanded the battlefield. Mining units of the British Second Army under General Gough laid twenty-one great mines, a total of 1,000,000 lb of high explosive, under the German lines and on 7 June they were exploded. The nineteen that went off shocked the German defenders and they staggered off the ridge as 2,266 guns and British, Australian and New Zealand infantry attacked. Prince Rupprecht ordered General von Armin first to pull back his Fourth Army, quickly regroup and then counter-attack. This blunted the British advance and by 14 June the German line was firm again, though the Allies held the ridge line. The Allies paid heavily for their success, with 108,882 casualties. German losses are estimated at 100,000 including 10,000 blown to pieces or buried by the enormous mine explosions.

MEUSE RIVER–ARGONNE FOREST: 26 SEPTEMBER–11 NOVEMBER 1918

Making an all-out offensive in the hope of ending the war, the Allied commander-in-chief, Marshal Foch, planned a gigantic pincer movement. French armies

Battle of Menin Road Ridge, near Zillebeke, 20 September 1917. Digging out wounded from the 13th Durham Light Infantry Regimental Aid Post which had been blown in by a shell. Some of the wounded suffocated. (IWM Q5979)

attacked from the west, and the American army under Generals Pershing and Bullard from the south. The German defences were 12 miles deep and the sector was commanded by Prince Freidrich Wilhelm and General von Gallwitz. In the first five days the French gained 9 miles, while the Americans progressed 5 miles along the Meuse heights and 2 miles in the more difficult forested area of the Argonne. Beginning on 4 October, the Americans won ground at heavy cost in several frontal attacks, and by 31 October they had cleared the Argonne Forest of enemy resistance. This was a 10 mile

Medical personnel at a field dressing station wait for their charges to be collected by a field ambulance.

advance. The French advance also began on 4 October and reached the Aisne river, a push of 20 miles. This grinding and costly advance continued until the Armistice, reaching Sedan on the east and Montmedy on the west. In terms of casualties the Germans had the better of the battle, losing 100,000 men to the Americans 117,000 and the French 70,000.

MONS: 23–4 AUGUST 1914

The Battle of Mons was part of the greater Battle of the Frontiers. The German Army, in its successful advance during the first weeks of the war, was attempting to break through the left flank of the Allied French and British armies and envelop large parts of them. The initial action was fought along the banks of the Mons–Condé canal, which was held by the British Second Corps, under General Smith-Dorrien, for a distance of 21 miles. The British commander-in-chief, General French, was absent when the battle started and played no part on his return. The German commander, von Kluck, also exercised little control over his own force, so that the German units stumbled one by one into the British.

The British dug in among the houses and slag heaps which covered the canal's twenty-one bridges. From here, the British infantry's shooting dominated the day; it was so fast and accurate that the Germans believed that they were facing massed machine guns. However, the German artillery was effective and it enabled its infantry to cross the canal and envelop a British regiment. The entire British line had to be withdrawn 2 or 3 miles south and a general retreat began, though screened by an effective rearguard. British casualties were 1,600 while those of the Germans were probably 3,000.

MONT ST QUENTIN, SOMME: 30 AUGUST–2 SEPTEMBER 1918

The Germans held in strength the key feature of Mont St Quentin, which dominated the fortress town of Peronne and much of the Somme river. While the fortified hill remained in enemy hands the Australian and British troops advancing eastwards against the slowly withdrawing Germans could make no progress. The Germans considered their positions, which were held by elite troops, to be impregnable. This was also the opinion of General Sir Henry Rawlinson, commanding the British Fourth Army. Lieutenant-General Sir John Monash, commanding the Australian Corps, believed that the hill could be taken, even though his battalions were so weak after lengthy combat that some were reduced to fewer than three hundred men. The Second, Third and Fifth divisions took part in the well-planned assault not only on Mont St Quentin itself but Peronne and Bouchavesnes Spur. The capture of Mont St Quentin by the Second Division is often regarded as the finest feat of the war. The Germans suffered 15,000 casualties to the Australians' 3,000.

NAMUR, BELGIUM: 20–5 AUGUST 1914

Namur was the last fortress city to attempt to block the advance of the invading German armies into France. It was defended by 37,000 Belgian troops, but the Germans had 100,000 men and 540 guns, some of them firing 2 ton shells. They battered Namur into surrender but by then the greater part of the garrison had been withdrawn and only 5,000 remained to be taken prisoner.

NEUVE CHAPELLE, FRENCH FLANDERS: 10–13 MARCH 1915

The British commander-in-chief, Sir John French, arranged an attack on the German lines at Neuve Chapelle in order to mollify the French commander-in-chief, General Joffre, who was indignant that the offensive on the Western Front was being 'neglected'. The British Army was short of shells and could not afford a preliminary bombardment so the attack by the British First Army, under General Haig, caught the Germans by surprise. For the first time in the war the British infantry broke the German line and took Neuve Chapelle, but Haig was reluctant to enter the gap his troops had made. While he waited for reinforcements, the German commander, General von Falkenhayn, brought up his own reinforcements. The gap was sealed and the British went on battering the German lines to no purpose. The British suffered 13,000 casualties to the Germans' 14,000. In effect, the battle set a precedent: initial success that led nowhere and attacks being made again and again when it was obvious that failure was irreversible.

LOOS (ALSO KNOWN AS THE BATTLE OF ARTOIS): 25 SEPTEMBER–8 OCTOBER

Loos was the British part of an Allied offensive in Artois, northern France. In this fight the British used poison gas for the first time, though so ineffectually that much of it blew back among their own infantry. Nevertheless, the British attack, under General Haig, gained some ground, as did the French operations in the Vimy Ridge area, under General d'Urval.

The French commander, General Joffre, had chosen Loos for the British attack without any study as to its suitability. It meant attacking across coalfields and through the obstacles posed by the ruins of thousands of miners' cottages. The British Secretary of State for War, Lord Kitchener, ordered General French to obey Joffre's directive. Haig, the army commander responsible for the attack, was confident of victory with the help of poison gas. On the first day the wind was blowing in the wrong direction and many British troops became victims of the gas. However, Haig's units gained some ground, broke through the German front line and dented the second line. Haig called for reserves, but General French had kept them far in the rear. During the confusion the Germans counterattacked and deadlock ensued.

Meanwhile, the French under General d'Urval had won some ground in the Vimy Ridge area. Then they stopped fighting. To satisfy Joffre, General French renewed the British attack until the offensive ground to a halt early in November. The casualties were appalling. The British lost 50,000 men to the Germans' 20,000. The French inflicted 120,000 casualties on the Germans but themselves suffered 190,000 casualties. One of the fiercest and bloodiest battles of the war, Loos achieved nothing.

NOYON–MONTDIDIER: 9–13 JUNE 1918

In launching his fourth offensive of 1918, General Ludendorff wanted to link his Amiens Salient with the Aisne–Marne Salient and so threaten Paris. On 9 June the first attack, under General Hutier,

AIF troops detraining at Poperinge, 30 September 1917. (Australian War Memorial)

drove back General Humbert's French Third Army, and on 10 June the second attack, under General Hoehn's command, smashed against the lines of the French Tenth Army, commanded by General Mangin. Hutier captured 6 miles of territory but his offensive was nevertheless blocked and the whole operation stalled. The Germans suffered 35,000 casualties to the French 15,000.

OURCQ RIVER: 6 SEPTEMBER 1914
The initial French counterattack, northeast of Paris, in the first Battle of the Marne.

PASSCHENDAELE: 9 OCTOBER, 12–14 OCTOBER AND 6 NOVEMBER 1917
This village in Belgian Flanders was a key point in the much larger battle for Ypres, which had begun on 31 July. The Allied

COURAGE, NOUS
SONGEONS À VOUS!

LE Field Maréchal Sir Douglas Haig.
Sous ses ordres les vaillantes
armées britanniques ébranlent les
troupes allemandes et libèrent la Bel-
gique du joug de l'envahisseur. Les
officiers et soldats des armées Britanniques ont la confiance la plus absolue
en leur chef et en son pouvoir de les
mener à une complète et glorieuse
victoire.

MOED, WIJ VERGETEN
U NIET!

VELDMAARSCHALK Sir Douglas
Haig onder wiens geleide het heid-
haftig Britsche leger de Duitsche troe-
pen uiteen slaat en België bevrijdt uit
de greep van den overweldiger. Offi-
cieren en soldaten hebben een volledig
betrouwen in Sir Douglas Haig's be-
kwaamheid om hen tot een volledige
en glorierijke zegepraal te leiden.

Field Marshal Sir Douglas Haig, the subject of a French postcard.

objective was to capture the whole of the Passchendaele–Broodseinde Ridge, control of which, Field Marshal Haig believed, would enable him to gain control of the Belgian ports. An attack on Passchendaele early in October did indeed provide a passage onto part of the ridge. Generals Gough and Plumer thought the offensive should now be called off but Haig continued with it, in the belief that possession of the entire ridge would give him a more easily defended line for the winter. The weather deteriorated and gave the final part of the

campaign its evil reputation for horror in the mud. The Australian divisions and the one New Zealand division were principally involved in the first two attacks, together with the Canadians in the third. Some Australians reached Passchendaele in the second attack and the Canadians took the ruins in the third. British and Empire casualties in the entire Third Ypres operation were close to half a million.

POLYGON WOOD, BELGIAN FLANDERS: 25–7 SEPTEMBER 1917
This battle was part of Third Battle of Ypres. In great strength, the Germans held the wood, which was less than 1,000 yd from the crest of the Broodseinde–Passchendaele Ridge. The Australian Fourth and Fifth divisions suffered 5,471 casualties in ousting the Germans from their strong defensive positions, which were centred on the prewar rifle range in the wood.

POZIÈRES, SOMME: 14 JULY–31 AUGUST 1918
The German positions in the ruins of the village of Pozières, 6 miles east of Albert, were very strong. Until they were captured the British offensive, which had begun on 1 July, could not develop. After some of the fiercest, most sustained fighting of the war, three Australian divisions – the First, Second and Fourth – captured the ridge on 4 August. They held it under artillery barrages and continual counterattack. In seven weeks

A Scots Guardsman gives a wounded German prisoner a drink during an attack, August 1918. (IWM Q6983)

they suffered 25,000 casualties, 33 per cent of their strength. German casualties were estimated at 40,000. On 26 July the Australians threw 15,000 grenades in possibly the longest bomb fight of the war. Many British and Canadian soldiers were also killed in the battle, which was not considered ended until 31 August.

ST MIHIEL: 13 SEPTEMBER 1918
The Germans had held the St Mihiel Salient, south-east of Verdun, since 1914. By late 1918 the Allies were pressing hard along much of the Western Front and the Germans planned a withdrawal

from the salient. But it could not get under way before the American First Army, under General Pershing, supported by French artillery and some French colonial infantry, struck the defences. The Germans lost 5,000 men killed or wounded, while 15,000 were taken prisoner. The Americans suffered 7,000 casualties; nevertheless the battle was one of the Americans' major victories.

SOMME RIVER I: 24 JUNE–18 NOVEMBER 1916
The traditional date for the beginning of this battle is 1 July, but this was merely the date on which the Allied infantry assault began. The artillery bombardment began a week earlier. The British front was 30 miles, the French 10 miles. General Haig's objective was to capture the German defences along the Thiepval–Pozières Heights and press on to Bapaume. The French, further south, were aiming for Peronne, which sat astride the Somme river itself. In the south the French, under General Fayolle, made immediate gains but the British Fourth Army, commanded by General Rawlinson, was cut down by concentrated machine-gun fire and in one day the British suffered 57,400 casualties, including 20,000 killed. The casualties were the result of inept British planning, the failure of the artillery to knock out the German positions and to cut their wire defences, and the sublime belief of the British generals that after the massive artillery barrage the infantry would

merely have to 'stroll over the fields' and occupy the German positions.

At the outset the Germans were led by Generals Falkenhayn north of the Somme, and Gallwitz to the south. As the Allies continued to make small but terribly costly gains the Germans brought in Field Marshal Hindenburg as commander-in-chief, with General Ludendorff as his chief-of-staff. On 15 September, at Flers, Haig used tanks for the first time in war but only eighteen of the thirty-six machines functioned. The fighting deteriorated into a battle of attrition and, in cold, drenching weather, Haig called off his offensive on 18 November. He was still several miles from Bapaume. The Allies had gained a mere 125 square miles at a cost of 425,000 British and 195,000 French casualties. Senior planning and leadership had been grossly inadequate. German losses are said, by traditional British sources, to be 650,000, but recent research shows this to be an exaggeration.

SOMME RIVER II: 21 MARCH–4 APRIL 1918

This battle is known to the Germans as *Kaiserschlacht* or 'Emperor Battle'. The Germans needed to gain a major victory on the Western Front before the Allies were stiffened by large numbers of fresh American troops, following the US entry into the war in 1917. General Ludendorff brought vast reinforcements from the quiet Russian front and after careful planning launched a massive assault against the British lines. Following a bombardment by

six thousand guns and a gas attack, three German armies – seventy-one divisions – jumped off along a 50 mile front south of Arras. They were the Seventeenth (General Bülow), Second (General Marwitz) and Eighteenth (General Hutier).

The onslaught was devastating and the British Fourth Army under General Gough, which consisted of only fifteen divisions, gave way. Next day Gough ordered his army to withdraw behind the Somme and as a result the British Third Army (General Byng) also pulled back. In four days the Germans captured 14 miles of territory. Ludendorff now concentrated his attack south of the Somme, where General Hutier commanded. On 17 March Montdidier fell to Hutier despite a combined French–British effort to hold it. The situation was so desperate that Marshal Foch was appointed chief coordinator of defence and Haig replaced Gough, some of whose troops had broken in panic, with General Rawlinson.

After a gain of 40 miles, the Germans came to a halt because of exhaustion and slowness of supplies. They had, in effect, moved too fast. Nevertheless, they had split the British and French, and they had threatened Amiens. The Allies suffered 160,000 battle casualties and lost 70,000 men as prisoners. The German armies lost 150,000 killed or wounded.

VERDUN: 21 FEBRUARY–18 DECEMBER 1916

This was the greatest battle of attrition in history, famous for the French pledge of

'*Ils ne passeront pas!*' (They shall not pass). The defences of Verdun consisted of twenty large prewar forts of reinforced concrete and forty smaller ones with interlocking zones of fire, and all were set in superb defensive country. However, the sector was vulnerable because the French High Command had stripped the forts of much of their armament, especially the heavy 155 mm guns. Following the fall of the Belgian fortress of Liège, the French had come to believe that forts could not withstand modern artillery. In any case, they needed heavy guns to support their operations.

The French began to reinforce the Verdun garrison in January. The Germans planned Operation Gericht to begin on 12 February but a blizzard blinded the gunners and their spotting aircraft, thus giving the French a week's respite. When the battle commenced, the German advantage was great – 1,400 guns in their main attack area to the French 270, together with seventy-two excellent divisions against thirty-four French divisions manning inadequate trenches. The German guns dropped shells on an 8 mile front for 12 hours; 2,400 shells fell on each football pitch-sized area of ground. Attacking with flamethrowers, the German infantry captured key positions: Fort Douaumont, 25 February; Hill 295 (Le Mort Homme) and Vaux, 29 May; Fort de Vaux, 6 June. The French repulsed two other violent assaults, on 23 June and 11 July. By now the French had suffered 315,000 casualties, the Germans 280,000.

The principal French commander until 1 May had been General Pétain, but he was replaced by General Nivelle, who launched a counteroffensive on 24 October. Largely under General Mangin's generalship, this operation won back much lost ground, including the forts of Douaumont and Vaux.

For the first time in history the outcome of a great battle depended on motor transport; 1,700 French trucks a day rolled along the Voie Sacrée (the Sacred Way) to sustain the defenders. The battle can be said to have ended on 18 December, when the French regained the front line as it had existed in mid-February. Even then, intermittent activity continued. Between them the French and Germans fired 40 million shells into Verdun battlefield. The French suffered 543,000 casualties, the Germans 434,000. For the French, Verdun was the great drama of the war and it still has a profound effect on the French people.

VIMY RIDGE: 9 APRIL 1917

The Germans captured Vimy Ridge, in north-western France, in 1914 and it became their strongest defensive position in the sector. During 1915 more than 115,000 French soldiers were killed or wounded in trying to retake the ridge, which is just north of Arras. The attack of 9 May 1915 made by the French Tenth Army, was particularly spirited and it actually secured a foothold on the ridge, but well-sited machine guns and an intricate enemy trench system proved too much for the French troops, who were thrown off the ridge. They tried again in June 1915 and again they were bloodily repulsed. A British–Canadian offensive was planned to recapture the ridge and no Allied operation on the Western Front received a more thorough preparation. The scheme called for miles of tunnels to be dug to enable attacking troops to reach their starting point without being shelled. After heavy British shelling on 9 April 1917, the Canadian infantry attack took one objective after another with unusual precision, even though the men were attacking in a snowstorm. Nevertheless, the Canadians suffered 10,600 casualties, including 3,000 dead. The Germans lost 20,000 men and were left without the heights which so dominated the plains of Artois.

YPRES I: 14 OCTOBER–11 NOVEMBER 1914

In mid-October 1914 the German armies moved towards Ypres, in Belgian Flanders, with the intention of outflanking the Allied French and British. At the same time the British, moving north from the Aisne, arrived at the town of Ypres with the intention of outflanking the Germans. The British were weaker in numbers and poorly led by the indecisive General French. They fought hard but at one time the Germans smashed a hole right through the British lines, creating a crisis in which cooks, batmen and others who rarely saw combat were hurried into action. The Allied defenders brought in fresh units by rail

faster than the attackers could move forward on foot and once more the Allied line steadied and held. The Belgians, on the extreme left, could hold their front only by opening the sea sluicegates and flooding the battlefield. The French rushed in strong reinforcements during the nine-day German offensive and General Foch then launched a great but vain counterattack on 20–8 October 1914.

The British had held onto a salient that poked 6 miles into the enemy front and the Germans could not dislodge them before heavy rain and snow ended the battle. The frontal assaults and massed artillery and machine-gun fire caused enormous casualties. The BEF lost 2,368 officers and 55,787 men at Ypres, heavier casualties than throughout the period since August. The British regular army virtually disappeared, leaving only a framework for the new mass armies that were to come. The German armies lost 130,000 men, the French 50,000 and the Belgians 32,000.

YPRES II: 22 APRIL–25 MAY 1915

Using poison gas for the first time, the Germans created alarm in the stricken British and French colonial defenders and quickly forced a 4 mile gap in the British Second Army line of the Allied front. The chlorine gas was an experiment and its success surprised the German commanders, who were slow to take advantage of their breakthrough. This gave the Second Army commander, General Horace Smith-Dorrien, time to rush

One way of trying to drag a soldier from the mud of Flanders.

A British trench in the Ypres Salient wrecked by enemy gunfire. Debris such as this was commonplace.

Canadian units into the gap. They held on during a second gas attack on 24 April. British counterattacks were costly in lives without much gain and Smith-Dorrien ordered a withdrawal to the edge of Ypres itself. His chief, General French, replaced him with General Plumer, who merely carried out Smith-Dorrien's plans to withdraw.

The Germans attacked several times but after give-and-take operations by both sides the Allied line held and the battle petered out on 25 May. Allied casualties were 60,000 to the Germans' 35,000. German use of gas was a tactical error. The prevailing winds of Flanders are westerlies so that when the British and French replied in kind the Germans suffered more heavily from gas than did the Allies.

YPRES III: 21 JULY–6 NOVEMBER 1917
The British commander-in-chief, General Haig, planned a major offensive for the second half of 1917, with the intention of capturing the Passchendaele–Broodseinde Ridge and continuing with a movement designed to reach the Belgian ports, which were occupied by the Germans. On 21 June British artillery opened a massive bombardment of the German Fourth Army front, which lasted for ten days. On 31 July the Fifth Army of General Gough attacked out of the Ypres Salient. It was supported by the British Second Army, under General Plumer, on its right and the French First Army on the left. A few miles of ground and 6,000 German prisoners were taken on that day. Heavy rain then filled the tens of thousands of shellholes and created a bog across much of the fighting area. The shelling had destroyed the intricate drainage pattern of the low-lying land and the mud that resulted impeded the attackers.

Fighting resumed on 6 August and Langemarck was taken, but Gough's units

A great pile of British 'toffee apple' mortar shells. They are still without their shafts, which slotted into the mortar's barrel. Wooden supports are attached to the bombs to stop them rolling about in transit.

could make little progress. On 20 September Plumer, using Australian troops as his spearhead, took Menin Road Ridge and gained another mile, despite German use of mustard blister gas. German tactics had changed. They relied on small machine-gun parties in shellholes, supported by concrete blockhouses which were virtually impervious to shellfire. Covered by such defences, the Germans delivered strong counterattacks before the British, Australian and New Zealand troops could consolidate the ground they had gained. The final action occurred on 6 November when Canadian troops stormed and held Passchendaele, 7 miles from Ypres. British and Empire casualties of 400,000 were not compensated for by the 65,000 they had inflicted on the Germans, and they captured only 9,000 enemy soldiers. However, the British effort had forced the Germans to move troops from other fronts to the Ypres sector and thus it had taken pressure off the French defence elsewhere. Third Ypres is often given the label of the Battle of Passchendaele, but Passchendaele was only part of the larger battle.

ZEEBRUGGE: 23 APRIL 1918

German submarines, though contained by the Allied convoy system, were still a menace to the Allies in 1918. The U-boats operated from bases at the Belgian ports of Zeebrugge and Ostend, and from the shelter of the canal port of Bruges, Admiral R.J.B. Keyes organized a raid against the bases, with the principal aim of blocking the port to prevent U-boats from using it. Seventy-five ships were to take part in the operation. With destroyer and submarine escort, the light cruiser *Vindictive* steamed into Zeebrugge and drew alongside the mole or central breakwater. Demolition parties disembarked and a British submarine loaded with high explosive was blown up against the lock gates, and two blockships were sunk in the channel. The base was not entirely blocked and to finish the job on 9 May the *Vindictive* was deliberately sunk against the lock gates. Forty German destroyers and submarines were unable to put to sea for several weeks. The British lost 635 men killed, wounded or captured.

CHAPTER SIX

THE AIR WAR

Air warfare was a direct product of Western Front trench warfare. Because of the trenches themselves, the barbed wire that protected them and the innumerable shellholes, cavalry was unable to fulfil its traditional role of scouting. Even if the horsemen had been able to negotiate the difficult ground they would have been large and easy targets for enemy riflemen and machine-gunners.

To obtain information about the enemy's movements behind his virtually impregnable trenches, the enemies turned to the still revolutionary aircraft for help. Few planes were available and few men had been trained to fly them but those that existed were rushed to the front, behind which small aerodromes had been established. At the time all that was necessary was a small, firm, smooth field. The pilots, soon to be accompanied by observers, were sent up as aerial scouts, with orders to observe and record every aspect of enemy military activity beyond the trenches. Their job was not to attack the enemy on the ground or to engage in hostilities in the air, though some pilots did so with revolvers, grenades and darts.

Observers were soon equipped with machine guns, but real aerial combat was not possible before the advent of forward-firing machine guns sychronized to fire through the spinning airscrew. The French were the first to achieve this, with a Morane Saulnier I, but the device was crude. The Germans, in the spring of 1915, developed an effective mechanism for the Fokker EI monoplane and it was this which brought Germany real dominance in the air. The role of these early fighters was to protect the scout planes but they quickly turned to the attack and, up to end of 1915, the Royal Flying Corps scout aircraft were the main targets.

As early as the latter part of 1915 the Germans had aces, such as Böelcke and Immelmann, the originators of the principles of air combat. The British and French, desperate for parity and then dominance, developed their own fighters and by the time the Battle of Verdun was raging, in the spring of 1916, and more definitely during the Battle of the Somme in the summer, the British and French held the upper hand. Their scout planes could move freely and this was essential if the enemy's fast-changing dispositions on the ground were to be countered.

The Germans responded at once. They reorganized the air force and introduced the D-type fighters so that by the end of 1916 they had wrested the initiative from their enemies. In 'Bloody April' 1917

A British pilot and his observer make a bombing run over an enemy town. The observer dropped his bombs by hand.

RFC pilots were being shot down in their hundreds.

In Britain, the designers and technicians worked nonstop to produce aircraft that could match those of the Germans, and the Sopwith Camel and the SE5, among other designs, were the answer. At first gradually and then more obviously the Allies took the initiative. In spite of the advent of the splendid Fokker DVII the Germans lost control of the skies. This had a great effect on the combat below, for the Allied fliers could now strafe and bomb the enemy troops.

Throughout the length of the Western Front, squadrons of British, American, Australian, French and Belgian aircraft took off from airfields that were generally close behind the front. Behind the Ypres Front, for instance, there were

121

RFC airfields at Hondschoote, Bray Dunes, Bergues, Ebblinghem, Proven, Abeele, La Lovie, Bailleul, Bavinchove and Coudekerke. Overall, hundreds of airfields were used, though not all at the one time. Once enemy aircraft began to attack an RFC airfield the squadron in residence moved to another one, perhaps to return to the original one when it was considered safe to do so.

For the troops below, dogfights were an absorbing spectacle, and there can have been few soldiers who did not witness several fights and see the losers come spiralling down in a crash. There was even fascination when a stricken pilot was seen to be trying to glide his plane to safety behind his own lines. Then there was a rush by troops in the area to save him. Sometimes a plane crashed in no-man's-land, where the pilot – assuming that he survived the impact – perished from small-arms fire. Nevertheless, many a pilot who scrambled from his plane and held up his hands in surrender was gestured safely into the enemy trenches.

The most famous crash was that of Baron von Richthofen, brought down on 21 April 1918 by the side of the Bray–Corbie road, near where an old brickworks now stands. Richthofen was dead before his plane crashed but the Australians, who held the territory at the time, were quick to reach it and to snatch souvenirs before a guard was put on the aircraft.

Modern visitors to the Western Front can barely imagine the amount of aerial activity that was taking place in clear weather. Each side felt it necessary to maintain continuous mastery of the air during daylight hours, so that the first flights were scheduled for dawn and the last came in just after dusk. As a matter of pride, the aces came in last.

The term 'ace' was applied to fliers who shot down five or more enemy aircraft, and it seems to have been first used by the French. Considering the large number of planes shot down overall, five kills was a low requirement, and the Germans stipulated that ten enemy planes should be shot down before an aviator could call himself an ace. Officially, the RFC/RAF did not adopt the practice because of the envy and resentment it might cause; for instance, how were 'probables' to be rated in a score? The requirements for claiming kills were strictly enforced and the statistics for the First World War are more reliable than those for the Second World War. The British had an enormous number of aces – 785 of them. The Germans had 364 (if we assume five kills to qualify), and the French 158.

In Britain very few of the Western Front aces had any publicity, Albert Ball being one of the exceptions. They were adequately, perhaps extravagantly, decorated but even then official policy was not to encourage publicity about them. In contrast, the French, Belgian, Italian, German and later the American aces were very public heroes. In Britain, even now, while many people might

The famous French air fighter Georges Guynemer stands by his plane talking to admiring generals. The stork was the emblem of his squadron.

know the names of the Germans Richthofen, Immelmann and Voss, the American Eddie Rickenbacker and perhaps of the Frenchman Georges Guynemer, they probably do not know their British and British Empire equivalents Mannock, Ball, McCudden, Barker and Collishaw.

Yet even in 1915–16 the name of Major-General Hugh Trenchard was known. In August 1916 Trenchard succeeded Sir David Henderson, who had been the first commander of the Royal Flying Corps in France. Trenchard had definite ideas about air strategy and tactics and insisted on the offensive. This

policy caused heavy losses – five hundred airmen during the First Battle of the Somme alone – but Trenchard's reputation grew, largely on the skill of his reconnaissance fliers. In January 1918 he was appointed chief-of-staff to the Royal Air Force, which took the place of the RFC in April of that year. Just before this change, Trenchard resigned, following quarrels with the first Air Minister, Lord Rothermere. He was succeeded by Major-General Sir John Salmond, who splendidly led the RAF during the final victorious months of the war. Trenchard returned to France to lead the Independent Force, Britain's strategic bombing group.

A striking feature of the Western Front, at least during clear weather, were the kite balloons, so called because, like any kite, they were at the end of a cord – actually a steel hawser. Kite balloons were invented by the Germans to provide observation for their artillery and to watch enemy activity. The French and British followed with their own similar balloons. A motor winch raised the balloons to an altitude of about 6,500 ft, from where the observer, cold and lonely in a wicker basket suspended below the balloon, carried out his work. He was in a splendid position to see all military activity, which he reported by telephone. During 1916 parachutes became available for the observer to drop to safety should his balloon he attacked by enemy fighters. While a balloon – or 'sausage' to British fliers – was a large target, it was protected by anti-aircraft guns and machine guns, and it had its own air cover. Some pilots became specialist 'balloon-busters'. Perhaps the most famous of them was the Belgian Willy Coppens.

The military balloon was 70 ft long and had lateral fins and a kite's tail for stability. Lieutenant Charles Watkins, a balloon observer in the RFC, told me that being aloft in a balloon was 'enthralling and exciting but terribly seasick-making'. He said that balloons were always winched down when the wind was stronger than 40 mph; conditions were then too rough for the observer to do his job.

The idea of dropping bombs from aircraft came in only slowly, but the French produced 6 in fléchettes or steel darts, which a pilot could drop onto his German adversary. It is doubtful if darts brought down a single enemy pilot. The British pilots dropped or threw infantry grenades at their enemies in the air. The real British pioneers were the fliers of the Royal Naval Air Service, with the 20 lb Hale bomb and a 112 lb naval bomb – not used on the Western Front by the RNAS. During 1915–16 the RFC used the same 112 lb bomb, the 20 lb Cooper bomb, a 230 lb bomb and a monster of nearly 600 lb. The Cooper was favoured for low-level runs against enemy trenches and emplacements.

The German air force began the war with the pear-shaped Carbonit bomb, with its fuse activated by a propeller. It was made in four sizes, the largest of which weighed 50 lb. In 1916 the Carbonit was replaced by the P.u.W bomb, with weights up to 2, 200 lb. The German fliers bombed rear areas of the Western Front with this torpedo-like bomb and probably caused more casualties and damage than the British did.

Leading Aces

BALL, CAPTAIN ALBERT

The first ace to become a 'hero' of the RFC and the British public, Albert Ball achieved much in his short career. Qualifying as a pilot in 1916, Ball flew two-seaters with No. 13 Squadron, among others, before he transferred to a fighter squadron, No. 11, in May 1916. He flew the Bristol Scout and the Nieuport 17, the aircraft in which he had his greatest successes. He was awarded the MC in July 1916 and the DSO in August. Back in England he was fêted as a young hero who daringly fought alone. His main tactic was to dive under an enemy plane and rake it with his Lewis gun. During 'Bloody April' of 1917 – a bad period for the RFC – Ball flew with No. 56 Squadron and shot down enemy planes with deadly efficiency. By 6 May his total number of kills was about forty-four.

Captain Albert Ball with some souvenirs of his victories. He had forty-three victories before being killed at the age of twenty.

The next day, at the age of twenty, he was shot down during a dogfight. The VC was awarded to him posthumously. He already held the DSO and two Bars, the MC, Croix de Guerre and Légion d'Honneur.

BARKER, MAJOR WILLIAM

A Canadian, Barker first flew as an observer/gunner and qualified as a pilot in 1917. He served with No. 28 Squadron on the Italian front and during this period was given command of No. 66 Squadron. His comrades said that he rarely went aloft without shooting down an enemy plane, and if this is somewhat exaggerated it nevertheless indicates his

deadly skill. Back in France, with No. 201 Squadron, he attacked a German two-seater when he was jumped by a formation of Fokker DVIIs and then ran into a formation of sixty Fokker DVIIs. During a nonstop action of 40 minutes, his Sopwith Snipe was hit three hundred times and he was badly wounded. Nevertheless, Barker shot down three enemy planes before the Snipe went out of control. Barker crash-landed and survived but this was his final fight. It led to his being awarded the VC to add to the DSO, MC and two Bars, Croix de Guerre, Légion d'Honneur and other foreign decorations.

BISHOP, LIEUTENANT-COLONEL WILLIAM ('BILLY') AVERY

A Canadian, Bishop flew operationally for only six months but was so successful that he became the second highest-scoring RFC ace. His career began with No. 60 Squadron in March 1917, when he shot down an Albatros DIII. During 'Bloody April' he won the MC and on 2 June he made an amazing single-handed attack on a German airfield and shot down three of the Albatros DIIIs that took off to intercept him. This exploit won him the VC, but this reckless, courageous man could not rest on his laurels and by August his score was forty-seven. After leave in Canada, he returned, as a major, to command No. 85 Squadron in March 1918. By 19 June, the date of his last fight, he had downed another twenty-five enemy pilots. It has been suggested that his recall to London was promoted by his superiors' fear that he could not possibly continue to survive. His final list of decorations: VC, DSO and Bar, MC, DFC, Légion d'Honneur, Croix de Guerre.

BÖELCKE, OSWALD

A German national hero from early in the war, Böelcke was as deadly as Bishop on the British side, but he was much more of a tactician. Always ready to search for his targets well over Allied territory, he had shot down eight Allied planes by the end of 1915. In the aerial mêlée over the battles raging at Verdun, he added to his score and his reputation, and in July 1916 he was given command of the Fokker-equipped Jasta II, one of the new fighter squadrons. He handpicked his pilots, one of whom was Manfred von Richthofen. Böelcke's teaching air tactics, expressed in the ten principles of *Dicta Böeckle*, became the professional bible of the German air force. On 15 October 1916, having flown five missions during the day, Böeckle ordered Jasta II aloft again. Another pilot collided with his plane, which crashed. Despite his death, two years before the war ended, Böeckle became known as 'the father of air fighting'.

COLLISHAW, LIEUTENANT-COLONEL RAYMOND

This Canadian, flying with the Royal Naval Air Service, is relatively little known, but with sixty confirmed victories he was the third-ranking RFC ace of the war and the highest-scoring naval pilot. His war career began in October 1916 with No. 3 Wing and he led B Flight, No. 10 (Naval) Squadron from its base at Furnes, Belgium. Collishaw had his flight's Sopwith Triplanes painted partly black, and as a result it became famous as the 'Black Flight'. The Germans feared Collishaw and his mostly Canadian comrades, and with good reason; between May and July 1917 the Black Flight shot down eighty-seven German planes. In this period Collishaw's own score increased to thirty-seven. In 1918 he commanded No. 203 Squadron, flying Sopwith Camels, and brought down another twenty enemy pilots between June and September. He was awarded the DSO and Bar, DSC, DFC and Croix de Guerre. His comrades were puzzled that he was not awarded the VC.

COPPENS, WILLY

A Belgian pilot, Coppens began his flying career late in 1916 but it was April 1918 before he scored his first victory, when he brought down a German fighter. He then built up a reputation as a 'balloon buster'. He attacked balloons at close range with incendiary bullets. In October 1918 German anti-aircraft fire brought down Coppens in a crash which left him crippled. He had shot down nine enemy aircraft and twenty-eight balloons, a total of thirty-seven, which made him the leading Belgian ace.

FONCK, CAPITAN RENÉ

This great French air warrior began his career early in 1915 flying two-seater scouts. He wanted to be a fighter pilot but his many applications for transfer were rejected until he achieved two confirmed victories. He was then posted to France's premier fighting formation – Groupe de Chasse No. 12 – Les Cigognes. Fonck's subunit was Escadrille SPA 103. In his first month with this squadron Fonck shot down four enemy aircraft. Probably the most professionally minded of all French pilots, Fonck delighted in his Spad fighter, and spent many hours practising marksmanship and studying the characteristics of Germany's warplanes and the tactics of their pilots. Never reckless, Fonck was calculating and cold-blooded in his work, and as a result he rarely needed more than a single brief burst of fire to dispose of an opponent. On two occasions, in May 1918 and again in September, he shot down six German aircraft in a single day. No other pilot of the war achieved this feat. His final triumph of the war took place on 1 November 1918, when he shot down a two-seater engaged in dropping propaganda leaflets over the French trenches.

The most difficult aspect of Fonck's remarkable career is assessing his score. With seventy-five confirmed victories he was the French and Allied ace of aces and second only to Richthofen as the war's supreme ace. Fonck claimed that his actual score was 127, which would place him as the war's number one. Since Fonck was not boastful, and as he kept his own meticulous records, it is possible that his score was actually well above that credited to him. At the war's end he had the satisfaction of being the greatest *living* ace; Richthofen, Mannock and many others were dead.

The much-decorated Capitan René Fonck, the leading French ace of the war.

GUYNEMER, GEORGES

The leading French ace, Guynemer did not look like a typical warrior. Unfit and frail, he somehow induced the Aviation Militaire to accept him as a mechanic in 1914 and in 1915 he qualified as a pilot. His first aircraft

In an unguarded moment, Georges Guynemer shows the strain and tension of being an ace pilot. This is believed to be the first publication of this photograph outside France.

was a Morane Saulnier scout, which he flew as a member of Escadrille MS3. On 19 July he shot down his first victim and his superiors, recognizing his extraordinary aggressiveness, posted him to a squadron using Nieuport IIs and later Spad VIIs. Guynemer attacked his opponents front-on and almost head-on, a brave but dangerous ploy. He was shot down seven times in his total of 666 flying hours. On 11 September 1917 he failed to return from patrol over Poelcapelle, Belgian Flanders. His aircraft and body were never found, though the Germans claimed to have shot him down. However, there is no proof of this. Guynemer, aged twenty-two when he died, was credited with fifty-four kills. A striking memorial to him dominates the central crossroads of Poelcapelle; it shows a great bird with folded wings, symbolizing, so it was said, death in the air and, according to some Frenchmen, 'a promising life interrupted'. Less poetically, it was his squadron's emblem.

IMMELMANN, MAX

One of the great aces of the 1914–16 period. Known as 'the eagle of Lille', the area in which he was based, Immelmann first observed for German artillery and then spent months as a scout pilot. When the Fokker EI fighter reached the German air force Immelmann took to it as if it had been specially made for him. On 1 August 1915 he shot down a French opponent and was awarded the Iron Cross First Class to mark the first victory by a pilot in an aircraft specifically designed as a fighter. He developed air tactics to a degree not previously achieved and is still known for his famous 'Immelmann turn'. This involved a half loop and roll which put him above an opponent who had attacked him from the rear. By spring 1916 he was a national hero with a tally of fourteen kills. He achieved only one more victory before, on 18 June 1916, he went down during a fight with FE2bs of the RFC's No. 25 Squadron. Some German historians claim that structural failure caused his machine to crash.

LUFBERY, RAOUL

Lufbery, number three among American fighter aces, first served with the French

Georges Guynemer, an ace of aces, in the cockpit of his Nieuport fighter. He looks composed enough here but note his expression in the photograph on the opposite page.

air force, as a member of Escadrille Lafayette. His career commenced in 1916 and he was instantly successful. The French decorated him with the Croix de Guerre and the British awarded him the MC. When the US entered the war, Lufbery was transferred to the new US Army Air Service as an instructor but in March 1918 he led the first American war-service patrol over enemy lines. In April he was given command of 94 Aero Squadron, flying Nieuport 28s. On 19 May a German pilot shot him down in flames, but after seventeen hits Lufbery's posthumous reputation was assured.

LUKE, FRANK

Luke specialized in shooting down enemy observation balloons and he destroyed fourteen of them. As they counted equally with enemy aircraft he had a final score of eighteen. This made him the second-ranking American fighter ace. An aggressive and pugnacious flier, Luke flew a Spad XIII with 27 Aero Squadron. On 30 September 1918 he engaged in a dogfight with Fokker DVIIs and was shot down. German soldiers called on him to surrender but Luke foolishly opened fire on them and was killed in the consequent gun battle. His record earned him the Congressional Medal of Honor.

MCCUDDEN, MAJOR JAMES

First a pilot of two-seater aircraft, McCudden was posted to the RFC's No.

29 Fighter Squadron in August 1916 and was given an Airco DH2s, in which he delighted. Still only a sergeant, he showed that he was a skilful and courageous pilot and his victory score mounted. Commissioned and decorated with the MC, McCudden became a flight commander in No. 56 Squadron and by April 1918 he had a kill tally of fifty-seven. McCudden had an advantage not possessed by most of his pilot comrades; he had begun service life as an air mechanic and he examined and sometimes serviced his own machine. In the RFC and RAF he was noted for his knowledge of tactics and his marksmanship, which was so deadly that his friends claimed that he could nominate which part of the enemy plane he would hit. In April 1918, McCudden, now a major, was awarded the VC and in July 1918 he was posted to command No. 60 Squadron. Amid cheers, McCudden took off to assume his new command, but moments after take-off his engine failed and the plane crashed. McCudden was killed. With a final tally of fifty-seven, McCudden was Britain's fourth-ranking ace. He held the VC, DSO and Bar, MC and Bar, MM and Croix de Guerre.

MANNOCK, EDWARD

After service with the Army, Mannock transferred to the RFC in August 1916 and received flying instruction from the ace James McCudden, among others. Early in 1916 he was with 40 Squadron, flying a Nieuport Scout, but he did not at first impress his seniors, some of whom said he lacked fighting spirit. That summer, however, thirty-year-old Mannock was awarded an MC and promoted to flight commander. By January 1918 he had sixteen victories and in May he was awarded the DSO; only two weeks later he was gazetted a second DSO. Promoted to major, Mannock was given command of 85 Squadron, with which he built up a reputation as perhaps the greatest RFC patrol leader of the war. On 26 July, just after shooting down another enemy pilot, Mannock was himself brought down by enemy machine-gun fire from the ground and crashed to his death behind German lines. His body was never found. On 18 July 1919 a posthumous award of the VC was gazetted. For many years Mannock was credited with seventy-three victories but in 1990 Shores, Franks and Guest, in their thoroughly researched *Above the Trenches*, reported that in a letter Mannock claimed only fifty-one. Their list indicates that Mannock flew two hundred sorties and that official records allow him forty-seven kills. One of the war's truly great fliers, Mannock was noted for his generosity in crediting some of his own kills to younger, less experienced pilots whom he was leading. His final distinctions were VC, DSO and Bar, MC and Bar.

NUNGESSER, CHARLES

This French ace began his military life as a cavalryman and he carried into the French Aviation Militaire all the dash that the French expected of their horsemen. He brought himself to popular

Two aircraft from a French squadron make a sortie over the trenches in 1918. (From a contemporary painting by François Flameng)

attention in 1914 when he captured a German staff car behind enemy lines – and narrowly avoided being killed by friendly troops who took him for a German. When he transferred to the air service he was engaged on scouting and bombing, but was impatient to fly fighters. Posted to Escadrille No. 65, he flew a Nieuport II, and though his score of hits steadily mounted, he had a series of serious mishaps. First he was injured while testing a new aircraft, which he damned in his report. Wounded during a dogfight over Verdun, he was commissioned and was ever more publicized for his feats. By December 1917 he had twenty-one kills.

Treatment of wounds kept him grounded until April 1917 and the German air force greeted his return with a challenge to single combat over Douai. Nungesser duly went up alone, only to meet six enemy fighters. Angry at this duplicity, he shot down two of them and put the others to flight. He was an angry wasp, one of his friends said. He was in such poor health that he should have been grounded but he insisted on being carried to his plane. After a period of rest he was planning to return to duties when he was badly hurt in a car crash. In August 1918 he was back in the air, to bring his tally to forty-five, the third-highest among French pilots. After the war Nungesser sought other challenges and disappeared during an attempt to fly across the Atlantic.

RICHTHOFEN, MANFRED VON: THE 'RED BARON'

Richthofen began the air warfare career which was to make him famous in May 1915, after he transferred from the cavalry to the air force. First an observer on the Russian front, he was then a member of a secret unit researching long-range bombing possibilities. Qualifying as a pilot at the end of 1915, he flew two-seaters and over Verdun he scored his first hit. He was still an unknown in August 1916 when Oswald Böelcke invited him to join a new fighter squadron, Jagdstaffel 2. On 18 September 1916 Richthofen, flying an Albatros DII, downed an FE2b. His biggest triumph of that year was his shooting down of the British ace, Major Lanoe Hawker on 23 November. In January 1917, with his tally at fifteen, Richthofen was given his first command, Jasta II.

Proud and ruthless and recognized on Böelcke's death as Germany's finest fighter pilot, Richthofen painted his aircraft red, hence the 'Red Baron'. Soon other pilots in Jasta II copied this practice. The RFC fliers called his Jasta 'the flying circus' but they certainly didn't laugh at these enemy fliers. By the end of April 1917 Richthofen had destroyed fifty-two Allied planes. Promoted to command a fighter wing of four Jastas, all equipped with the Fokker DrI triplane, Richthofen became a scourge. At the turn of the year his score was sixty-three and he was the most famous warrior in Germany.

In statistical terms he was living on borrowed time and on 21 April 1918 he

A dogfight between French and German aircraft above a raging battle, *c.* 1916

was killed by a bullet fired from the ground by an Australian Lewis-gunner. His death took place during a dogfight he was having with some Canadian pilots of the RFC and this led to their claiming, understandably but mistakenly, that they had shot him down. With a final score of eighty kills, Richthofen was the war's ace of aces. The AIF buried him in the civil cemetery at Bertangles, near Amiens, and a firing party gave him a salute of honour.

RICKENBACKER, CAPTAIN EDWARD

Rickenbacker was nothing more than General Pershing's driver when he went to France in 1917, but he was hell-bent on flying and took lessons in his own time. Accepted as a flier in 94 Aero Squadron in March 1918, Rickenbacker was a member of Raoul Lufbery's formation on 19 March when it became the first American patrol to fly over German lines. He shot down his first victim on 29 March and by the end of April, with four more hits, he was an ace. Sickness kept him out of the air until September when he returned to duty as the Squadron's commanding officer. In his Spad XIII he became a menace to the Germans and by 11 November and the end of hostilities he had twenty-six confirmed kills, including four balloons. His friends claimed that his real score was much higher. As the leading American ace, Eddie Rickenbacker was awarded the Congressional Medal of Honor.

VOSS, WERNER

Voss first flew as an observer during the Battle of the Somme, pestered his superiors for pilot training and joined Jasta II in November 1916. Almost at once he brought down a BE2c and by February 1917 he had a score of twenty-two. Other officers were already speaking of him as another Richthofen. During the Nivelle Offensive he destroyed several French planes, and in July 1917 he returned to the Somme, this time as commander of Jasta X, although he was only twenty years of age. His number of kills rose to forty-eight on the morning of 23 September 1917. Later that day, in his Fokker DrI, he ran into a British air patrol from No. 56 Squadron, led by Major James McCudden. In the dogfight, which was witnessed by many troops on the ground, Voss was killed and his plane crashed. McCudden and other fliers were unstinting in their praise for Voss' skill and courage. In the German air force he was considered second only to Richthofen in ability.

PRINCIPAL WARPLANES

THE DH RANGE (BRITISH)

Various Airco DH planes served over the Western Front, one of the most famous being the DH2, which was used by the first single-seater fighter squadron, No. 24 Squadron. It appeared in France in January 1916 and was so successful that other squadrons adopted it. The DH2 took part in 744 recorded combats and gained forty-four hits, mostly against the Fokker biplanes, which had threatened to become the scourge of the skies in 1916.

Despite its success, the DH2 was still only a pusher and it was replaced by the DH5, a tractor biplane with a speed of nearly 105 mph, very fast for 1917. Pilots had no great trust in it except as a ground-attack machine with its four Cooper bombs. It was used during the Battle of Cambrai. Meanwhile, the DH4, capable of 145 mph, had arrived as a high-speed bomber, but it also had a Vickers gun and a Lewis gun, for pilot and observer respectively.

The DH6 came into use later in 1917 but it was not liked by pilots, some of whom called it 'the flying coffin'. Others referred to it as the 'dung hunter', because, they complained, it tended to dive and sniff. With an underpowered engine, the DH9 was inferior to the DH6, but it was the stock aircraft for nine or ten squadrons on the Western Front and was in use until the end of the war.

ALBATROS (GERMAN)

Various models of the Albatros were in service but undoubtedly the most successful was the Albatros DIII, known to British pilots as the 'vee-strutter' from the shape of the struts which linked its two wings. With two Spandau machine guns, a ceiling of 18,000 ft, speed of 110 mph and flight endurance of 2 hours, the DIII was so formidable that all the German forward squadrons dedicated themselves to it. Richthofen flew an all-red DIII. The heavy losses suffered by the RFC in 'Bloody April' of 1918 were caused by the DIII pilots. Later Albatros types were not as successful as the DIII.

ARMSTRONG WHITWORTH (BRITISH)

Armstrong Whitworth produced the FK3 and FK8, the former being used by the RFC as a trainer. The FK8 or 'Big Ack' – to distinguish it from 'Little Ack' – reached the RFC in France in 1917 as a scout and bomber. On the Western Front it was found to be efficient in a ground-attack role. The pilot fired a Vickers mounted on the fuselage while the observer in the rear seat operated a ring-mounted Lewis gun. During 1917 and 1918 only five squadrons were equipped with the FK8, which is surprising considering its popularity among pilots, two of whom were flying the model when they won Victoria Crosses.

AVIATIK (GERMAN)

Made in Germany and Austria, the Aviatik was produced in several models and used as a scout, bomber, fighter and escort. The CIII was the type mostly seen over the Western Front, usually flying with reconnaissance squadrons. The observer could move his Parabellum machine gun from one side of the cockpit to the other in earlier models, and later there were two guns fixed to a tail on either side. The crew of unarmed two-seaters felt secure when escorted by a CIII so armed.

AVRO 504 (BRITISH)

An Avro 504 had the unlucky distinction on 22 August 1914 of being the first RFC aircraft to be shot down. However, this did not damage its reputation and in November three Avros bombed the Zeppelin sheds at Friedrichshafen, on Lake Constance. This was the first organized long-range bombing raid of the war. Rapid advances in aircraft design made the Avro obsolescent in 1916, but the RFC kept it on as its most-favoured trainer. Records show that 8,340 Avro 504s of at least ten continually improving types were produced during the war.

BE AIRCRAFT (BRITISH)

Various BE scout and fighter aircraft flew over the Western Front from as early as August 1914. The first of them were important in reconnaissance duties and the BE2e was probably the first with anything like defensive armament. The BE12 was supposed to be the RFC's answer to the German Fokker, but it was left to the BE2b to fulfil this role. It was the crew of an FE2b that shot down the famous Max Immelmann in June 1916. It was a rare success for the British plane. The FE8 had a disastrous day on 9 March 1917 when Richthofen, leading a formation of Albatros DIII, engaged nine FE8s, sending four down in flames and damaging the others. Nevertheless, the FEBE series did good work when better planes were not available. They were generally known as Royal Aircraft Factory products but several manufacturers made BEs.

BRISTOL F2A AND F2B (BRITISH)

A two-seater fighter-scout biplane, the Bristol reached the Western Front in December 1916 and soon acquired the nickname of 'Brisfit'. The Bristols' presence there was concealed until April 1917, when they were introduced as a surprise weapon. The German fliers were not impressed and Richthofen's 'circus' shot down four Bristols on 5 April during the Battle of Arras, and even more in the following days. Revising their tactics, the Bristol crews flew their aircraft as if they were single-seat fighters. The pilot operated the Vickers as he zoomed in against an opponent while the observer fired his Lewis purely for defence. From then on the Bristol became a scourge for German fliers and 3,101 machines were in service by November 1918. The Bristol Scout was less famous but the 160 or so that reached the Western Front did fine work. Early Bristol Scouts were unarmed and the pilot carried a revolver or rifle. When an above-wing Lewis gun was fitted to the plane some pilots had remarkable successes, notably Lanoe Hawker, whose

feat in shooting down three German two-seaters earned him the VC.

FOKKER AIRCRAFT (GERMAN)

The Fokker, designed by a Dutch engineer of that name, was the most famous of all the German aircraft which operated over the Western Front in 1918. Probably the best of the long series of Fokkers was the DVII, a single-seat biplane. It could climb to 15,000 ft in a mere 16 minutes and it had a flight endurance of 90 minutes. Fokker pilots said that the DVII was easy to fly, that the pilot had excellent visibility in all directions, and that the plane was manoeuvrable. With two fixed 7.92 mm Spandau machine guns synchronized to fire through the propeller, the DVII was an outstanding fighter. The first of the type to reach the front equipped Richthofen's Jagdgeschwader 1. The DVII intrigued Allied pilots with its ability to 'hang in the air' at an angle of 45 degrees, a posture that would have taken other aircraft into a spin. It was the strength of the 185 hp BMW engine that enabled the Fokker to 'hang' in this way. While 2,000 Fokker DVIIs were ordered, only 760 were delivered.

The Fokker DrI was designed by Fokker specifically to counter the danger posed by the Sopwith Triplane. Quite small, the DrI had a manoeuvrability, and a pilot who knew how to handle the two independent Spandau machine guns was a formidable opponent. Werner Voss, flying a DrI in Jasta I, scored ten victories in September 1917. Richthofen's Jasta I was equipped with the DrI in mid-October, but his Jasta was the only one to retain confidence in the aircraft. Richthofen himself had faith in it and he was flying a DrI when he met his death in April 1918.

Fokker E-type single-seater monoplane fighters were successful for the German air force from mid-1915 to mid-1916.

JUNKERS (GERMAN)

One of the best-known aircraft names of the latter part of the war, Junkers were produced in several types. The Junkers DI was the first all-metal warplane to appear over the Western Front. A single-seater fighter, the DI was a fast climber, and had large numbers been available in 1918 it could have affected the outcome of the war. The two-seater CLI was excellent in fighter and ground-attack roles, but it too appeared too late to influence events. The Junkers JI had the all-metal construction that became a feature of all Junkers. Coming into service in 1917, the JI was an infantry-support aircraft, perhaps the best of the war.

MORANE SAULNIER AIRCRAFT (FRENCH)

Monoplane and biplane Morane Saulnier types were a feature of the Western Front skies from 1914. The best known was the Morane Parasol (or Type L), a two-seater that the French Aviation Militaire used extensively for scouting. The RFC had some Parasols in service as early as December 1914 and used them on bombing missions. In such a plane Flight Sub-Lieutenant Warneford of the RNAS destroyed a Zeppelin over Bruges on 7 June 1915 and won a VC. The Parasol was the first fighter to be fitted with a forward-firing machine gun capable of firing through the propeller arc. The designer was the French pilot and engineer Roland Garros, who promptly shot down three German aircraft. When he himself was shot down on 19 April 1915 the Germans discovered the secret of Garros' success and adapted it for their own fighters. RFC pilots said that some models of the Morane Saulnier were difficult to handle, and perhaps for this reason the Parasol was not popular with the British.

NIEUPORT AIRCRAFT (FRENCH)

The French produced at least ten different models of the Nieuport fighter, which helped to make many pilots famous. In 1916 it greatly assisted the Allies to win the battle of the skies over Verdun in 1916. The Nieuport 12 was one of the most versatile aircraft to be used on the Western Front; it was a combination fighter, scout and light bomber. The Nieuport 17, or 'Superbebe', was the most outstanding of all, and from May 1916 it was in service with French Aviation Militaire, the RFC and the RNAS. Fast and manoeuvrable, 'Superbebe' appealed to several aces, notably Albert Ball, Billy Bishop, René Fonck, Georges Guynemer and the Italian leading ace, Francesco Baracca.

Bishop's thirty-six hits while flying the Nieuport say much for the plane's performance. With a maximum speed of 102 mph, the Nieuport could climb to 6,000 ft in seven minutes, a remarkably fast rate of climb at the time. A later version of the aircraft, the Nieuport 28, was even faster at 122 mph, and the Americans used it in 1917–18. It was the fighter most favoured by Eddie Rickenbacker, the leading American ace.

PFALZ AIRCRAFT (GERMAN)

Various Pfalz models served the German air force well as single-seat fighter-scouts. One of them, the Pfalz DXII, had a 180 hp Mercedes engine that could drive the plane at the formidable speed of 180 mph and lift it to the impressive altitude of 18,500 ft. This gave the pilot the scope for high cruising and deadly diving and, being strongly built, the Pfalz did not shed its wings as some other aircraft did. Allied airmen encountered many Pfalz-equipped Jastas in the early part of 1918 and considered them almost as dangerous as the Fokker formations.

SOPWITH AIRCRAFT (BRITISH)

The Sopwith 'Camel' was the most famous British fighter of the war and the most successful of all First World War fighters. Its pilots shot down 1,294 enemy aircraft. Officially known as the FI, the plane was affectionately known as the 'Camel' because of the hump-shaped cover for the breeches of the twin Vickers machine guns. The 'Camel' was amazingly manoeuvrable, and those fliers who admired it said that it could make right-angle turns. It was first in action on 4 July 1917 and many aces readily took to it, including Barker and Collishaw. The Sopwith factory and its contractors built 5,410 'Camels' as well as several other Sopwith models. In the training squadrons the 'Camel' had a high accident rate, but those pilots who mastered 'the beast' swore by it.

SPAD VII (FRENCH)

More Spad VIIs – 5,600 – were built than Sopwith 'Camels', which was an indication of their popularity. The French produced the Spad and their aces adopted it, among them René Fonck and Georges Guynemer. With a speed of 132 mph it was 17 mph faster than the 'Camel' but less manoeuvrable. It also had only one Vickers machine gun but experienced pilots said that in a Spad they needed only one gun. In eight minutes they reached an altitude of 12,000 ft and from that height they came down like lightning on the enemy. Three British squadrons were equipped with Spads, as well as Belgian, American and Italian squadrons. The Americans preferred the Spad XIII to any other fighter and equipped their finest squadrons with it.

CHAPTER SEVEN

PRINCIPAL WEAPONS

The principal weapons were the same for all armies. Every officer was armed with a revolver or pistol, while nearly all other ranks carried a rifle and a bayonet. Some other ranks, such as machine-gunners, carried a revolver for their personal protection, as it was impossible to carry a heavy part of a medium machine gun in addition to a rifle, and difficult to carry a light machine gun and a rifle.

Light and medium machine guns were commonplace by the latter part of 1916. The lighter machine guns were considered platoon weapons, while the medium machine guns were managed by machine-gun battalions or by the machine-gun platoon of an infantry battalion.

Most infantrymen carried a few grenades, but some members of a section, platoon and company were officially the bombers. Most infantry battalions had a bombing officer, who commanded the bombing platoon. In past times these men would have been called grenadiers.

Many types of guns were used on the battlefield, from mortars and howitzers to field guns, medium guns and heavy artillery. Mortars and howitzers lobbed their projectiles with a high trajectory; all the others fired their shells on a flat or a curving trajectory.

French marine artillerymen and their massive railway guns.

Swords were carried by officers in the first months of the war but it soon became clear that in the conditions of combat prevailing on the Western Front, they were useless. Bayonets were of much more use.

Gas was freely used as a disabling weapon, but the sub-machine gun, so commonplace in later wars, was still in its development stage.

RIFLES

Throughout the war the rifle was the predominant weapon for all the armies fighting on the Western Front. Sub-machine guns had not been invented, and the crews of medium machine guns such as the Vickers, Maxim and Hotchkiss could not keep pace with the infantry in advances. Light machine guns, such as the Lewis, did keep up but often ran out of ammunition. Grenades were used in vast numbers but many soldiers became tired from carrying them and the supply quickly ran out. Trench mortars were a valuable front-line weapon but they were heavy to carry, as were the bombs they fired, and they were not always available. For all these reasons the rifle and bayonet was the ever-present weapon. Wherever a soldier went, so did his personal weapon.

The basic system for all rifles was the same, being based on a bolt-action operation together with a magazine capable of holding a number of rounds. Some rifles had removable magazines but most were part of the rifle, with cartridges being inserted in clips of three to six rounds. Magazines, however, could hold more than this. There was no such thing as automatic or semiautomatic action until 1918. The soldier pushed each and every round into the breech with his rifle bolt and ejected each spent cartridge case by withdrawing the bolt. Of course, there were variations. For instance, the eight rounds of the early Lebel had to be loaded individually until the French Army introduced a box magazine.

Under combat conditions the performance of the various rifles was roughly similar. The maximum range – that is, the point at which the bullet fell down – was 3,500 yd. British soldiers were taught that it was a waste of ammunition to fire a rifle at a specific target more than 600 yd away. Much nonsense has been written about rates of fire. Certainly it was possible for a soldier to fire twenty rounds a minute from a .303 SMLE, but only if he was attempting to alarm the enemy by volume of fire. Aimed 'rapid fire' varied between eight and twelve rounds a minute, according to the level of training and experience. The famous fifteen aimed rounds a minute managed by the British regulars of 1914 was a remarkable achievement.

The bullet fired from a German Mauser, known as *spitzgeschoss* (or 'pointed bullet'), was more streamlined and had a flatter trajectory. The 'S' bullet reached a height of only 6 ft in a flight of 700 yd to hit a target, while a Lee-Enfield bullet rose to 10 ft. The lower trajectory of the *spitzgeschoss* resulted in marginally more effective accuracy, an important factor for soldiers employed as snipers.

LEE-ENFIELD RIFLE

Virtually every British soldier on the Western Front was armed with this splendid weapon, known officially as the Short Magazine Lee-Enfield (SMLE) Mark III. Its name came from a combination of the name of James Lee, an American designer, and the Royal Small Arms Factory at Enfield, near London. A trained soldier could fire twelve well-aimed shots a minute or twenty more roughly-aimed shots, despite the need to reload the ten-round magazine. Possibly the best standard service rifle of the First World War (and the Second World War), the Lee-Enfield or one of its variants was sturdily reliable, even in Flanders mud.

LEBEL RIFLE

The French Army's standard infantry rifle in 1914–15. Officially the Fusil modèle 1886, the Lebel was an 8 mm weapon with a serious defect – its eight rounds were loaded, nose to tail, in a tubular magazine under the barrel. Loading was slow because of the risk of one round hitting the primer of the cartridge in front, causing an explosion. For a time it was the only rifle to fire smokeless cartridges, but this asset did not prevent the Lebel from being largely replaced by the Berthier rifle, which was loaded from clips, in the fashion of the British rifle.

BERTHIER RIFLE (FUSIL D'INFANTERIE MODÈLE 1907, TRANSFORMÉ 1915)

The Berthier was not only clip-loaded, but had different sights as well as variations on the Lebel bolt mechanism. Because of the large demand, some Berthiers were made in the US by Remington. The Berthier's drawback was that the magazine held only three rounds, a marked tactical disadvantage. The 07/15 was redesigned to take five rounds and the result was the Fusil modèle 1916, which was loaded from a six-round clip or charger. While the Fusil modèle 1916 was being produced a carbine version was being made, the Mousqueton modèle 1916. All in all, the French Army had problems in finding the ideal Western Front rifle.

MAUSER RIFLE

In various models, the Mauser Gewehr 98, firing a 7.92 mm cartridge, was the German Army's basic rifle throughout the war. It had been in service since 1898 so it was already well tested when hostilities began. Despite being incapable of rapid fire, because of its bolt arrangement, and because of the limitations of a five-cartridge magazine, it was nevertheless accurate and dependable. Fitted with an optical sight, the Mauser became a sniper's rifle and as such was much used on the Western Front.

LUGER PISTOL P08

This famous German 9 mm pistol was used not only by officers – a common impression – but by many other German soldiers, and about two million were issued. Technically, the Luger was the

Parabellum*-Pistola modell 1908, or P08 for short. The seven-round magazine was held in the pistol's butt. The weapon was recoil-operated and was considered reliable and accurate, even though it had a barrel of less than 9 in. A variation of the Luger, the Parabellum M17, reached the front in 1917. More a machine carbine, the M17 had a longer barrel and the magazine held thirty rounds. The Luger became a desirable trophy among British and Empire troops.

MAUSER C96 AND C10 PISTOLS

The Mauser was used almost as widely as the Luger in the German Army. It was large, bulky and awkward but it fired a powerful 7.63 mm or 9 mm round to a useful combat range and its appearance appealed to German soldiers. It also had a wooden holster which could be fitted to the weapon to turn it into a shoulder-fired short rifle. The Mauser model 1910 was also produced in large numbers.

WEBLEY REVOLVER

The Birmingham firm of Webley and Scott was established in the 1830s but it was half a century before the firm bought the 'Pryse patent' for a hinged frame that itself extracted the six spent cartridges

*Parabellum literally means 'pistol for war', and under the name Parabellum it was widely adopted as a military pistol. The term '9 mm parabellum cartridge' came to mean one of much greater power than the smaller 9 mm cartridge.

from the revolver. The British Army adopted the Webley-Pryse model in 0.442 calibre and called it the Webley mark I. In 1899 the calibre was changed to 0.455 (11.6 mm), by which time the marks had reached IV. This was the version which was so reliable in the First World War. Large numbers were turned out to arm all British and Empire officers and some NCOs and men, such as those manning Vickers machine guns. It was a tough, durable weapon; it had to be since it was often dropped into mud. The heavy slug was a man-stopper even when it was not fatal, but much practice was needed for accurate shooting as the weapon jumped on firing. While it was a good weapon, many British officers preferred to use a captured Luger, which they said had a longer range.

FRENCH PISTOLE REVOLVEUR MODÈLE 1892

This was the standard French service pistol and it was produced not only by a large number of French state factories but by Belgian and Spanish makers. It was often referred to as the 'Lebel' or 'model d'Ordonnance'. In appearance it was similar to a Webley, with a six-round chamber, but it fired an 8 mm round. The big difference was that while the Webley snapped open for reloading, the chamber of the modèle 1892 swung out. The modèle 1892 or variations of it can still be found on French battlefields, rusted but otherwise intact.

MACHINE GUNS

MAXIM MACHINE GUN

Hiram Maxim, an American, designed in 1884 the weapon which bears his name, and Britain was the first country to use it. Astonishing though it might seem, the British Army's leaders could see 'no real use' for a fully-automatic machine gun. However, the German Army recognized its potential and, as the Machineengewehr 08, produced the gun in quantity at the Spandau factory. Hiram Maxim's concept was simple and clever. The gas produced by the explosion of the powder in each cartridge created a recoil which continuously operated the entire gun's mechanism. Water cooled and belt-fed, the Maxim had a nominal rate of fire of six hundred rounds a minute.

This was the weapon which the Allied troops feared and which caused so many casualties among them. When the war began the German Army had 12,500 MG 08s in service, while the British and French had only a few hundred equivalent machine guns. This large number, which was to grow to more than 100,000, indicates the tactical importance that the Germans gave to the

The German G8 machine gun, the scourge of many a battlefield. (IWM Q35445)

weapon. The gun, with its sledge mounting and spare barrels, weighed about 62 kg. The canvas or fabric ammunition belts held 250 7.92 mm cartridges, and its possible rate of fire was 300 rounds a minute.

The crews of the MG 08s were hand-picked for their intelligence and steadiness, given special training and treated as an élite. A version of the MG 08, the MG 08 15, was much lighter than the MG 08 and came into service in large numbers in 1918. In a semimobile role, these guns were concentrated at various points to cover the German Army withdrawals of the latter half of 1918.

From the beginning, German tactics in the use of the medium machine gun were superior to those of the Allies. This can be seen from a simple comparison. In the British Army the few guns available in the first years of the war were attached in sections to individual battalions. The German Army maintained separate machine-gun companies to support those with infantry battalions. More than this, the regimental commander – the CO of three battalions – retained command control over all the machine guns. He could then group them as a battery, a method which proved to be much more effective than battalion command of guns.

VICKERS GUN

The British Army knew a good deal about the Vickers gun because it had been the first to use the Maxim, the Vickers' parent. However, the British had not perceived the gun's potential as the Germans later did, and in 1914 only two were alloted to each infantry battalion. The Machine-Gun Corps was formed in October 1915 and equipped with Vickers, which, in the estimation of many troops, was the 'Queen of the battlefield'. A water-cooled gun, the Vickers fired standard .303 ammunition – as used in the rifle and light machine gun – fed from a fabric belt. It was mounted on a weighty tripod when used by infantry and it was also used in tanks and aircraft. In 1916 the Sopwith 1½-strutter became the first warplane to be fitted with a Vickers.

By 1918 the machine gun was dominant on the battlefield, simply because by then there were so many of them and quantity in machine-gun issue was vital to compensate for the ever-weakening ranks of infantry battalions. By mid-1918 some of them, with an establishment of nearly a thousand, were down to a few hundred men. It was supposed, in 1918, that a machine gun was the equivalent of eighty rifles, a rough indication of its massive fire power.

The rapidity of fire from a machine gun was terrifying to those facing it. Six hundred rounds a minute was common-place and this was battlefield practice, not merely a theory. The Germans in particular had great supplies of ammunition at any one machine-gun post, so that they could maintain heavy fire for long periods. British and Empire soldiers who overran enemy posts were amazed at the quantity of ammunition stocked in them. From 1917 on, when armies had machine-gun corps, the fire plan for an assault specified a machine-gun barrage in the way that artillery fired a barrage.

The rapidity of fire caused acute heating of the barrel. It could be cooled in one of two ways – by air, with radiating fins attached to the barrel, or by water circulating in a jacket around the barrel. A Maxim used nearly a gallon of water, which reached boiling point after six hundred rounds had been fired. Thus, the jacket had to be regularly re-filled. This could have been difficult or even impossible in combat, but a simple system was introduced to provide water. The water jacket had a steam vent and condensed steam was run off through a tube into a water can. The resulting water was used to refill the jacket. Gun teams carried a spare barrel too. As a gun barrel soon became worn, resulting in inaccurate firing, every gun team carried spares.

An American 14 in railroad gun involved in fighting in the Argonne region, September 1918 (IWM Q81616)

The gun, ammunition and water supplies were heavy enough, but the heaviest part of the equipment was the tripod or 'sledge' on which the gun was mounted. A Maxim team consisted of four to six men while the Vickers team was always six-strong until casualties occurred. No. 1, the principal gunner, carried the tripod, mounted the gun and fired it, apart from being responsible for its general operation. No. 2 carried the gun and fed the ammunition belt into the weapon; Nos 3 and 4 carried ammunition and No. 4 in addition maintained the supply of water into the jacket. Nos 5 and 6 kept the gunpit or post in good condition and protected the others by scouting and observation. Of course, all numbers were trained in the use of the gun and there were many occasions when only one man remained alive and fit enough to keep the gun in action.

Guns could not be quickly resited, mostly because of the weight of ammunition which, for a section of two guns, amounted to 6 cwt.

Medium machine guns firing on fixed lines were ideal for covering a front at night. During daylight the gun was aligned on the target for the night while the sights were set on some nearer, visible object, such as a lamp whose light could be seen only on the side facing the gun. The gun itself was kept pointing towards the target. The gunner kept his sights on the aiming mark, confident that his bullets were hitting the target he could not see. This method was used to fire at a spot from which the Germans were known to emerge for raids, for instance, or a break in the wire defences. Very often machine-gunners would be called on to give overhead supporting fire to their own infantry, but only after they had ranged onto the area to be covered so that they could observe the strike. In this way they hoped that their fire would not hit their own troops, though accidents often happened.

Many British and Empire infantrymen referred derisively or bitterly to machine-gunners as 'the shoot, shit and scatter boys'. They were convinced that the gunners, having done a shoot, quickly changed position before enemy artillery came down on them, leaving the infantry to suffer the shelling. The slur was unjustified.

During the British attack on High Wood on 24 August 1916 British troops fired more than one million rounds from ten Vickers guns during a 12 hour period. This is just one of many indications that the Vickers was a reliable weapon and that infantry could depend upon it. A barrel was worn out after ten thousand rounds – an hour's continuous firing – so the High Wood gunners must have had an ample supply of spare barrels or used whatever barrels they had to the point where the guns were wildly inaccurate.

LEWIS LIGHT MACHINE GUN
Designed and developed in the United States, the Lewis became the principal British and Empire light machine gun. In 1915 each battalion had only four Lewis guns but by 1917 every infantry section

had its specialist Lewis-gunner and his number two. The battalion had a total of thirty-six guns. The gun weighed 26 lb, the magazine held 47 or 97 rounds of .303 in ammunition, and it could fire up to 500 rounds a minute, providing the ammunition was to hand. In fact, it was generally fired in short bursts. The RFC/RAF used the Lewis as the standard weapon for the observer in a two-seat aircraft; it was also seen on the Western Front in tanks and armoured cars. It is remembered principally as an infantry weapon; troops in action felt infinitely less protected when their section Lewis gun was knocked out of action.

HOTCHKISS LIGHT MACHINE GUN

The French Army's 8 mm infantry light machine gun was the Hotchkiss. Much was expected of this weapon, which appeared in 1909, but it was too heavy, at 25 lb, for mobile warfare. When trench warfare began, trouble with the gun's magazine feed gave it a poor reputation. However, it proved to be useful in aircraft, where it was invariably fired in short bursts. It was also successful as part of tanks' armament. The British produced the weapon as the .303 Hotchkiss Machine Gun Mark I; the Americans knew it as the Benet-Mercié Machine Rifle.

A massive 400 mm shell is hoisted up, ready to be rammed into the gun breach. The big French guns rivalled those of the Germans in size.

HOTCHKISS MACHINE GUN 8 MM MODEL 1914

The French Army's standard heavy machine gun. This large, tripod-mounted gun weighed 52 lb, which was indeed heavy. Later models used metallic strip ammunition belts holding 249 cartridges, which made it almost impossible for a gun-team to maintain the weapon's cyclic rate of fire of 600 rounds per minute. It was mostly used in static positions where supplies of ammunition were at hand. American units also used the Hotchkiss model 1914.

ARTILLERY

FRENCH 75 MM FIELD GUN

The most famous field gun of the war on the Western Front, the 75 mm – le Canon de 75 – had the astonishing rate of fire of 20–25 rounds a minute, even though it lacked any form of automatic reload. Despite this shortcoming, the .75 was advanced for its time, with a hydro-pneumatic recoil system which gave it stability during firing. Because it did not 'buck back', as so many field guns did, the crew could operate quickly. It had a range of 7,500 yd, further than the British 18-pounder could fire. As with everything else in the French Army, the 75 mm had been designed for offensive action rather than defensive action, but the army remained devoted to the weapon. From 4,000 in use in 1914, the number grew to 17,600 by 1918.

GERMAN 77 MM FIELD GUN

The Feldkanone 16, produced by Krupp, was the German Army's answer to the French 75 mm, and it was probably as good. Firing high explosive, shrapnel and gas shells, it had a range of 11,264 yd and, like the 75 mm, its trajectory was

A French 75 mm gun battery in action, firing at Germans caught in the open.

An Australian soldier ready to fire a 'toffee apple' bomb from a mortar in a trench gunpit.

flat. German soldiers depended on the 77s for quick response to Allied infantry attacks.

BRITISH 18-POUNDER FIELD GUN
Throughout the war, the 18-pounder – which the army had been using since 1904 – was the standard field gun of the British Army. The gun was the close-support weapon for the infantry, and with a maximum range of 6,525 yd it was generally close behind the lines and sometimes in the lines. In specification,

the gun had a calibre of 3.3 in, weighed 2,821 lb and had a single-action breach.

On the Western Front, the British regarded one gun to each 30 yd of front as adequate in 'normal' times; for an offensive the distribution became one gun to 10 yd. For an offensive, the French tried to maintain one gun for 15 yd, one field gun each 15 yd, a medium or heavy gun every 30 yd and for counter-battery fire, one every 35 yd. The Germans used even more guns. For their breakthrough offensive in March 1918, on a 50 mile

Lancashire Fusiliers in a front line trench. A Lewis gun team clean their weapon while their mates stay alert. Note the gas alarm horn and wind vane.

front they used the following weight of guns *per mile*: 92 field guns, 31 field howitzers, 14 medium howitzers, 14 heavy guns, 7 heavy howitzers and 4 super-heavy howitzers. German artillery did not fire on the entire 50 miles at any one time. Artillery doctrine called for certain sections of the Allied line to be crushed with double this number of guns while a neighbouring section was untouched – until the following shoot when it too received double ration.

'THE PARIS GUNS'

The German guns which bombarded Paris between March and August 1918 were not styled 'Big Bertha' or 'Long Tom', as is popularly believed. The

Unexploded shells found by the author in one day, in 1994, on a small farm field on the Somme. Those with narrow driving bands just above the base are German. The two on the right, with the driving bands removed, are British.

German Army knew these 21 cm monsters as Lange Kanone, while the soldiers called them 'William's guns'. They were not accurate and perhaps they had no need to be since the intention was merely to terrorize Paris. This did not happen and damage from the comparatively light shells was insignificant. The French say that the guns fired 320 shells into Paris, while German records mention 367. There was also a 'Long Max', a 15 in naval gun which shelled Dunkirk.

Sub-Machine Guns

In 1918 the Germans introduced the only true sub-machine gun of the war, the Bergmann MP 18. The 'MP' was designated a machine pistol, but with a 32-round drum magazine and a rate of fire of 540 rpm, it was a genuine sub-machine gun in the modern sense. Only limited numbers had been produced before the war ended. About the same time the Italians introduced the Villa Parosa, a double-barrelled weapon for use in aircraft, but I can find no evidence that it was used by the army.

THE BAYONET

The use of the bayonet in combat during the First World War is generally supposed to have been very limited. I believe that this view is mistaken and that it is based on an extension of the obvious truth that more soldiers were killed by bullets and shells than by the bayonet. This does not mean that the bayonet was rarely used, only that it was relatively little used.

Certainly everybody concerned with treating casualties, from stretcher-bearers on the field of battle right down the medical chain to base hospitals, saw more bullet, shrapnel and shell-shard wounds than those from bayonets. But while many soldiers with projectile wounds lived long enough to be borne from the battlefield, most of those with bayonet wounds did not; they generally bled to death quickly before bearers could reach them.

Nearly all of the several hundred infantry veterans of the First World War whom I knew said that they had taken part in bayonet fighting. On interrogation, some of them admitted that they had not actually crossed bayonets with an enemy but they insisted that they had been in a position to do so before their enemies either surrendered or ran.

My question, 'Did you actually wound an enemy soldier with your bayonet?' often elicited nothing more than an awkward shrug or a half-smile, but a considerable number of soldiers said they had 'stuck the bayonet in', though some

A raiding party bombs along an enemy trench with grenades. Sometimes the bombers moved ahead of the bayonet men. Note the man with a trench periscope further back.

men would have been reluctant to admit that they had *not* fought with the bayonet. In addition, my questions do not constitute a scientifically based study, but anecdotal evidence suggests to me that the bayonet was used at close quarters more frequently than is commonly believed.

I suppose that no student of the Western Front would dispute that the bayonet often had a decisive influence in winning an engagement, simply because it terrified one side or the other.

A further point must be made. In training, many instructors taught recruits that having overwhelmed an enemy position, they should bayonet any wounded German still capable of fighting. The instructors said, 'A wounded enemy on the ground can be more dangerous than a prisoner of war. A standing prisoner is disarmed but an enemy lying on the ground may be concealing a pistol or grenade, even a rifle. He might shoot you in the back as you press on or he could kill one of your mates.'*

Some modern historians have quoted veterans as saying that the bayonet was used primarily for toasting, opening tins, scraping mud off uniforms and boots, digging small latrine holes and poking a brazier. It could also be used, when stuck into the side of a trench or the wall of a billet, as a hook for holding eqiupment and clothing.

'The spirit of the bayonet' cropped up frequently in the training camps or 'bullrings' of Étaples, Bailleul and Amiens. Here, the instructors quoted from the training manuals, which said, 'In an assault the enemy should be killed with the bayonet. Firing should be avoided for in the mix-up a bullet, after passing through an opponent's body, may kill a friend who happens to be in the line of fire.' The manual urged instructors 'to inculcate the spirit of the bayonet into all ranks so that they go forward with that aggressive determination and confidence of superiority born of continual practice.'

'Go straight at an opponent with the point threatening his throat and deliver the point wherever an opportunity presents itself,' the manual advised. Soldiers were taught that the 'vulnerable points' of an enemy's body were the throat, left breast, right breast, left groin, right groin. In training, they made practice thrusts at these points. There was much to fault in this training, as must have become evident to many soldiers, after they had been in a few actions. Surprisingly, the manual and style of training were never amended. For instance, a bayonet driven into the breastbone was often difficult to wrench out, thus giving the wounded soldier's comrades a chance to kill his attacker. A bayonet in the groin was so agonizing that a stricken man would grab it fiercely in an attempt to pluck it out and not let go. Some British and Australian veterans recalled that they had to detach the bayonet from the rifle in order to carry on the attack.*

---

*Under instruction from a First World War veteran in 1940, I was told, 'Take no chances, bayonet the bastards as you pass.' This senior NCO maintained that it was easier to bring oneself to bayonet a fallen enemy than to shoot him. I believe this to be true.

*The author evolved a style of bayonet fighting in 1943 which became the subject of a training film. I taught that the most vulnerable parts of an enemy soldier's body were his hands, as they held his rifle. By slashing his fingers or sticking the bayonet point in his hand I could disable him. He might then surrender. If not, he could easily be dealt with by bayonet or butt.

British soldiers wait in a communication trench for their turn to move forward.

it may be conceded that the bayonet was more valuable as a psychological weapon than a physical one, especially in the hands of soldiers not averse to using it, such as the Australians, but this admission is not evidence that its physical use was insignificant.

The Germans used more types and variations of bayonets than all their enemies combined, though this does not indicate a greater willingness to use the weapon. One reason for the great variety of bayonets in German hands is that they made special adaptors so that captured foreign bayonets could be fitted to the Gewehr 98 rifle. Allied propaganda made much of the 'saw-back' bayonet, which had a double row of teeth on the back edge. The propagandists said that this savage-looking weapon was a measure of 'Hunnish barbarism'. In fact, the bayonet was issued to pioneers and engineers as a saw, though no doubt, given the opportunity, they would have used it against enemy soldiers.

The German Army had a long infantry bayonet at the start of the war but soldiers criticized it as unwieldy and from 1916 all bayonets were shorter.

During a raid that took soldiers into an enemy trench the bayonet was useful, though because of the narrowness of most trenches the movements had to be thrusting rather than slashing. In general,

GRENADES

A grenade is a hand-bomb used by infantry. All armies were ill-provided with grenades at the outbreak of war but trench warfare quickly demonstrated

their importance. Until better models became available soldiers fashioned grenades out of tins that had held jam, meat or tobacco. Into them was packed explosive, nails, glass and chunks of iron.

By 1915 the production of grenades was prodigious. The German standard model was the *Steilhandgranate*, a steel canister filled with explosive and attached to a handle, generally 14 in long. The soldier tugged a length of cord running through the handle; it operated a friction igniter which activated a detonator. The British used several models of grenade, including one with a metal handle, before settling for the Mills bomb or HE (high explosive) No. 36 grenade. When it exploded it broke into numerous hurtling segments. In a trench or dugout a Mills bomb had a devastating effect.

The French used various cylindrical and spherical grenades as well as models fastened to sticks. All the armies used rifle grenades. A shaft fitted down the barrel of a rifle, from which it was projected by a bullet and, in a later development, by a cartridge which, when exploded, created intense gas pressure up the barrel.

Soon after the outbreak of war the British Army put a rifle grenade, known as the Hale, into service. The Hale consisted of a 4 oz explosive charge in a tube inside a cast-iron casing. The grenade exploded on nose impact and the iron casing fragmented at high velocity. A thin steel rod protruding from the base fitted into the rifle barrel and stabilized the grenade in flight. Use of a Hale from a rifle so seriously damaged the barrel that the weapon could not be used for

normal shooting. Despite this drawback, the Hale was in service until late 1917.

All the many designs of hand grenades had the same basic construction. This consisted of a metal casing packed with explosive and provided with a means of ignition and detonation. Some contained pieces of iron, nails and glass to add to the effect of the bursting case. Some writers refer to hand grenades containing shrapnel and experiments were indeed carried out in Britain, France and Germany using the type of shrapnel found in shrapnel shells. However, there was never a shrapnel grenade in common use. The killing and wounding effect came mostly from the segments of the bursting case and, in confined spaces, from the blast.

All the armies experimented with time fuses and impact fuses. The time fuse was the more reliable. In one method the detonator was struck smartly on a strip of matchbox striker, which many bomb-throwers had tied around their sleeve. The British and Turkish cricket-ball grenade operated in this way. Another method of ignition was the friction fuse, which was activated by a cord hanging outside the grenade. The Germans used this in their 'stick' or potato-masher grenade, though the cord was held in the stick or throwing handle by a screw-on cap until the soldier was ready to throw it. Most effective of all was the spring-loaded igniter, which was activated when the user pulled a safety pin from the grenade. A spring was then released which forced a plunger against a percussion cap, igniting the fuse which then exploded a detonator. The British Mills bomb, the HE No. 36 grenade, employed this method.

In comparison, the impact fuse was crude. The thrown grenade had to fall on its plunger, which fired a detonator. The manufacturers helped this process by designing the casing with the heaviest metal around the plunger. Gravity was supposed to do the rest. Gravity was assisted by attaching streamers so that the grenade hit the ground plunger first. The streamers' primary function was not to give the grenade a greater range, as is so often believed. The Germans had a grenade that had eight chances of going off; shaped as a discus, it had eight projecting lugs and exploded when any one of these lugs hit a target. The German soldiers disliked it because it had to be handled with great care.

Early in the war Britain and France made grenades known either as the racquet or hairbrush, although butter-pat more realistically describes their shape. The explosive was attached to the pat and was activated by a pull cord.

Rifle-grenades were much used on the Western Front because they had a longer range – up to 180 yd. In 1914–15 the grenade was welded to a rod which was pushed down a rifle barrel and fired by a blank cartridge and then by the powerful ballastite cartridge. Rifle barrels quickly deteriorated from having rods fired from them. In 1917 the British and French

introduced a cylindrical cup attachment, known as the cup-discharger, which was fixed to the muzzle of the rifle. The grenade, a Mills bomb with safety pin removed, was placed in the cup and fired by the ballastite cartridge.

The French Viven-Bassières or VB had a crude though apparently effective mechanism. The grenade had a hole through its core that matched the hole of the rifle barrel. When the soldier fired a bullet it passed through the grenade and activated a fuse; simultaneously the gases in the barrel caused by the cartridge explosion launched the grenade into flight. The cup-discharger could give a grenade a range of 400 yd and it could therefore be lobbed into enemy support trenches as well as the front trenches.

Throwing hand-grenades was a skill learnt by training. Because it was physically demanding and dangerous, the fittest and bravest men were selected as bombers. After instruction and practice they were expected to lob at least half their missiles into a 10 ft by 4 ft trench at 30 yd, though some men could throw further than this. Grenades were bowled and rarely thrown. Bowling, cricket-style, ensured a greater height and a more vertical drop, whereas a thrown grenade could so easily hit the enemy parapet and explode ineffectively. Bombers were also taught how to use the grenade from a kneeling or lying position.

All infantrymen were trained in throwing grenades but relatively few became specialists. The British and

A German soldier in late summer 1914. Note the type of grenade, the fuse of which was ignited by pulling a cord.

Empire armies instituted nine-men bombing teams, comprising an NCO, two throwers, two carriers, two bayonet men as protectors and two spare men to take the place of casualties. Some of these teams were immensely successful in trench raids. The throwers led the way to lob bombs into an enemy-held trench bay; the bayonet men then rushed into that bay to finish off any enemy who might still show fight. In those few seconds the throwers would be resupplied by the carriers to attack the next bay.

Many bombers were killed or wounded by their own bombs. At least three VCs were awarded to soldiers who, to save their comrades, threw themselves on to live bombs they had dropped and were killed in this act of courage. I have to say that I do not regard this self-sacrifice as an act worthy of a VC but no more than might be expected from somebody whose own carelessness had imperilled his comrades. In 1918 an Australian soldier was awarded the Albert Medal for such an act, in which he lost his life. This seems to me to have been an appropriate posthumous award.

The British and Empire armies used an estimated fifteen million hand-grenades on the Western Front. If this number seems to be an exaggeration, reflect that in a one-hour fight at Pozières an Australian battalion threw fifteen thousand grenades. Some men needed weeks to recover from the physical exertion and strain.

GAS WARFARE

Chemical weapons were used experimentally in August 1914, first by the French, who fired tear-gas grenades. The Germans are usually accused of having started gas warfare but in fact they were the second users, when they fired shells treated with a chemical irritant at Neuve Chapelle in October 1914. In January 1915 they fired tear-gas shells against the Russians on the Eastern

Women ambulance drivers were frequently seen on duty behind the lines on the Western Front. The haversack this girl is wearing contains her gas respirator. (*Illustrated London News,* 24 November.1917)

Front. The date 22 April 1915 marks the first major use of poison gas, when the Germans released chlorine gas against French positions near Boezinge, in the Ypres Salient. In all, 520 gas cylinders discharged 168 tons of chlorine, which the wind carried to the enemy troops, in this case mostly French colonial infantry, and to some extent British and Canadian infantry. The men had no gas masks and did not at first understand that the greenish vapour approaching them was poisonous. Five thousand men died and another ten thousand were disabled. A break in the line occurred but the

Germans were not ready to exploit it and fresh troops blocked the gap.

Frantic countermeasures by the Allies produced crude protection in the form of handkerchiefs soaked in bicarbonate of soda solution or urine. Gradually, masks of various kinds were developed and improved steadily until the box respirator was issued late in 1916.

In the meantime, the British used chlorine gas at Artois–Loos on 25 September 1915. The tactic failed because the wind blew the gas back against the British troops preparing for an assault. Since the prevailing winds on

The hell of Verdun. An alarm warns of a gas attack.

the Western Front were westerlies, the Germans suffered more from gas casualties than the British and French did.

The Germans were generally one step ahead of the Allies in chemical warfare developments. In July 1915 they fired chlorine in artillery shells. In December 1915 they used a choking gas, phosgene, and in mid-1917 they struck with mustard gas, which was all the more deadly because it was odourless and almost colourless. Winds did not affect the shell-delivered mustard gas, which settled as a fine spray before it could be blown very far. Many Allied soldiers suffered from severe burns to the skin and the respiratory system. More than one million men became gas casualties during the war, though many of the injuries were slight.

Some gases were lethal, such as phosgene, a respiratory irritant. Some irritant gases caused the eyes to water, induced sneezing or produced blisters. Sometimes tear gas was sent over to make

it difficult for the victims to put on their masks, and while they were thus helpless a deadly poison gas was fired by shell into their positions. The Germans used nearly 70,000 tons of gas, the French 37,000 and the British 25,000 tons.

While eighteen separate gas variants were used, these were the main ones:

Benzyl bromide: Strong German lachrymator (tear gas)
Bromacetone: The Allies used this potent lachrymator
Chlorine: Both sides employed this insidious respiratory irritant, which produced spasms that could be fatal
Chloropicrin: A stronger form of chlorine, used by both sides from 1916. The Germans called this gas 'Green Cross 1', a term that became infamous
Cyanogen compounds: Used in Allied shells, cyanogen was supposed to leave no permanent damage, though this would have been disputed by those German soldiers who caught a heavy dose and died.

ARMOUR ON THE WESTERN FRONT

If the Western Front were famous or infamous for nothing else, the use of tanks for the first time in war would have given it historic significance. But as with other weapons, such as machine guns, the modernizers and innovators on the Allied side had a hard time convincing

the military and political chiefs that armour would be useful.

However, armoured cars were in use on the Western Front in the first months of the war. The Belgians, French and British armies skirmished with them against German cavalry patrols. The

A French armoured car races through a German-occupied town and opens fire on the startled enemy soldiers. This painting by Georges Scott, completed in 1918, shows how the war of movement had replaced that of the trenches.

Belgians, using Minerva sporting cars armed with a Hotchkiss machine gun, were particularly enterprising and courageous in this form of open warfare, especially around Antwerp, which the Germans were besieging in 1914.

Allied armoured cars also attacked infantry outposts but trench warfare put a stop to all that; wheeled vehicles could not operate across trenches. Germany and its allies, as well as the Russian Army, made little effort to find a way of breaking through wire and storming across trenches, but a few far-sighted and determined British army officers and

engineers saw the need for some kind of assault vehicle that could surmount the obstacle of trenches and barbed wire and save soldiers' lives. In Britain one of the earliest pioneers was Lieutenant-Colonel Ernest Swinton, who was an official army observer. As early as October 1914 he suggested that armoured caterpillar tractors should be built as a way of breaking through trench defences, but GHQ and many other executive and supervisory groups ridiculed the idea.

Meanwhile, in November 1914 the French suggested a mechanical wire-cutter mounted on a tractor, but

An artist's realistic impression of a French tank about to crush an enemy trench.

development of this system was scrapped early in 1916.

Swinton persisted with his ideas and gained the support of Winston Churchill, together with that of naval officers and a banker, Albert Stern, a service officer who became the financier of an official research and study team.

Churchill's role was important. As First Lord of the Admiralty he had made the Royal Navy responsible for operations along the Belgian coast, and he ordered Commander Samson to use squadrons of armoured cars to function as a guerrilla force to protect the airfields from which naval warplanes were trying to bring down German Zeppelins. It was this experience which brought in the navy as the developers of the tank, which it considered a 'land ship'.

In June 1915 the indefatigable Swinton produced a specification for his new war machine. With a speed of 4 mph it must be able to climb a 5 ft obstacle, cross a 5 ft trench and be proof against small-arms fire. It should be armed with two machine guns and a quick-fire cannon, and it would need a crew of ten. With various modifications this is what the first tank designers, Walter Wilson and William Tritton, produced.

By now some senior officers, and of course Churchill, realized the potential importance of the machine, so a code-

A French tank crushes all before it in 1918. An artist's impression.

name was needed to hide its development from the enemy. The great casing looked as if it might be a water carrier, so in December 1915 the code label evolved was 'tank'.

In January 1916 the first combat tank, tested in front of important officials, convinced them that here was an answer to the Western Front stalemate. The Minister of Munitions, David Lloyd George, at once ordered more tanks. Meanwhile, the French, who as allies knew about the British experiments, were still not convinced of the tank's usefulness. The French answer to all battlefield problems was more and yet more artillery. But the French too had their exponent, Colonel F. Estienne, and he convinced the dull commander-in-chief, General Joffre, that a tracked vehicle carrying a gun might be a battle-winner. An initial order for 400 Schneiders and 400 St Chamonds was placed.

The first British tanks came off the production line in June 1916, with the navy supplying the crews, though before long the army assumed control. On 15 September 1916 Captain H.W. Mortimore made history when he took a tank D1

An artist's impression of an early British tank under fire. At that period rear wheels were needed to steer the cumbersome vehicle.

into action at Delville Wood. Soon after this, thirty-six tanks led infantry in a successful attack against German defences at Flers. The Germans were terrified.

Battle conditions were, appalling for the crews in the heat and choking fumes but they stuck to their task and some earned decorations. Private A. Smith became the first 'tanker' to be so recognized when he was awarded the MM for gallantry at Delville Wood on 15 September.

Tanks did not at first live up to the high hopes held for them, largely because High Command was all too eager to use them before they had been adequately developed. At Bullecourt in April and May 1917 the Australians felt so let down by tanks that they lost confidence in them. Also in April, the French used 128 tanks at Chemin-des-Dames but many broke down and all came to grief on the shell-torn ground.

In July British GHQ foolishly committed tanks to the Passchendaele offensive, against the advice of tank officers, and they sank deep into the mud, as they were bound to do. The crews continued to fight from their ditched machines and one crew fought off German infantry for nearly three days before they withdrew to their own lines after all of them had been wounded.

A British tank lies hopelessly ditched in a communications trench in 1918.

The French were probably the first to fight a wholly successful tank attack when ninety-two of their machines were committed at Malmaison. The result was not spectacular but at least it showed what might be achieved. That potential was fulfilled on 20 November 1917 at Cambrai, when the entire British Tank Corps was engaged and breached 12 miles of the German front, inflicting 10,000 casualties on the Germans, who lost 123 guns and 281 machine guns. The great success was nullified because GHQ did not have the troops ready to exploit the breach.

However, the British experience at Cambrai reinspired the British and French in their tank development. In addition, the American Army for the first time recognized the significance of tanks. Even more important at the time, the German Army, which had been so advanced in all other methods of waging war, now hastily went into tank production. It formed its first tank section in January 1917.

On 24 April 1918, thirteen German tanks, mostly A7Vs, successfully engaged British and some Australian infantry at Villers Bretonneux, east of Amiens. During this action three British Mark IVs took on three A7Vs south of the town and drove them off. Soon after this history-making tank-versus-tank engagement an Australian pilot called up seven British Whippet tanks to charge German infantry.

The most significant event concerning tanks occurred on 4 July 1918, when General John Monash, commanding the Australian Corps, used tanks, infantry, artillery and warplanes in the first true all-arms coordinated assault of the war to win a remarkable victory at Le Hamel, between Villers Bretonneux and the Somme river. Monash said that it was not the business of infantry to win battles at great cost to themselves by simply charging enemy machine guns. After artillery preparations, the tanks should spearhead an assault with the infantry in close support. Similarly, it was slow and wasteful for soldiers to carry masses of heavy stores and ammunition to the front positions; carrier tanks could do this job. Monash's victory at Le Hamel, achieved in only 93 minutes, showed all Allied commanders how to use tanks to their best advantage.

On 23 July thirty-five British tanks supported a French division in a successful operation at Moreuil in a direct copy of Monash's Le Hamel operation. In the same period, 18–26 July, the French Army used 336 Schneiders, St Chamonds and Renaults to support French and American infantry at Soissons.

On 8 August 1918 tank warfare on the grand scale reached the Western Front. A massive 604 Allied tanks took part in the great Allied advance on a 20 mile front. Here they not only breached the enemy line, as at Cambrai, but with Whippets penetrated all the German lines to allow the infantry to fan out. For a brief time it seemed that the Germans might collapse.

Some tank exploits were amazing. During the 8 August offensive a Whippet named 'Musical Box' (Lieutenant C.B. Arnold) fought a lone 10 hour action against the Germans. The crew destroyed a gun battery and a railway train, as well as scores of trucks and wagons. In addition, they killed many Germans being rushed up to fill the breach. 'Musical Box', its driver dead, was then hit and set on fire. The furious Germans beat up the rest of the crew but they survived their captivity.

The American Army had by now formed a Tank Corps, using Renault tanks. Nearly two hundred of them were used in the Battle of the St Mihiel Salient. The US Tank Corps was in action again during the Battle of Meuse–Argonne, 26 September–5 October 1918, but it lost heavily in tanks and men, largely because the force lacked

the experienced control of the British and French tank units. The American crews were brave but they darted all over the battlefield and made themselves ideal targets for German field artillery.

Lord Kitchener, Minister of War in 1914, had said that the machine proposed by Colonel Swinton was nothing more than 'a pretty mechanical toy'. By 1918 this 'toy' was showing signs of dominating the battlefield. The so-called male tank, with its cannons, and the female tank, armed with machine guns, powerfully supported the infantry and broke the morale of the enemy, when efficiently used. In 1918 tanks had become so important on the Western Front that a repeat of trench warfare could never occur.

A Mark I (Male) tank crossing a British trench on its way to attack Thiepval, 25 September 1916.

CHAPTER EIGHT

DECORATIONS AND MEDALS

Awards for bravery and distinguished service were important in maintaining morale in all the armies involved in the First World War. A decoration is quite separate from service medals, such as those medals worn with pride by millions of British and Empire service personnel. Few men in any battalion or other fighting unit were awarded a decoration. This can be seen on the Western Front by walking down the rows of headstones in a large military cemetery. Only a handful of men have the emblem of the VC engraved on the stone, while DSO, DCM and MM are infrequently seen on a stone after the name of a dead soldier.

The British decorations described here are those relevant to the army, the RFC/RAF, the Royal Marines and the Royal Naval Division. All fought on or above the Western Front and all were eligible for the same awards. The RAF did not have its own distinctive decorations until after the war, while the Royal Navy's decorations were mostly awarded for bravery and distinguished service at sea.

The British, French, Belgians and later the Americans awarded their decorations to service personnel in one another's forces. Sometimes this was done on a ration basis, so that a commanding officer of a battalion would be advised to put forward the names of, say, ten of his soldiers to be awarded the Croix de Guerre. Similarly, the British would grant ten Military Medals to a French unit. They were issued un-named; that is, the name of the foreign recipient was not engraved on the rim. When awarded to British and Empire personnel, most British decorations carried the name of the recipient regardless of rank. The DCM and MM were also always name-engraved to British and Empire personnel but the MC, an officers' award, was not named in the British Army.

Many men hungered for a decoration and it is very likely that some had an award in mind when they embarked on a dangerous mission. Units were collectively pleased when one of their members was awarded a very high decoration, such as the VC.

A study of decorations and the citations which accompanied them reveals remarkable anomalies. Sometimes an MM citation seems to warrant a VC and a few VC citations implicitly suggest that a lesser award was more appropriate. Some gallant deeds were not rewarded at all.

Colonel Rowland Feilding, the CO of two separate infantry battalions and one of the most experienced officers of the war, confessed that he detested decorations because of the disappointment and bitterness felt by some men, especially young officers, who believed that they deserved recognition. On the other hand, a decoration was sometimes awarded to an officer or soldier for doing nothing more than his duty.

The anomalies were so well known that it was said of many an officer, 'He was awarded a good MC', meaning that it was well deserved. The award of combat clasps would have obviated much of the criticism about decorations. A soldier of any rank who wore the clasp *Loos 1915, Pozières 1916, Vimy Ridge 1917* or *8 August 1918* would have felt adequately recognized. The clasp would have proved his presence and suggested his courage in the respective actions.

Another problem, at least in Britain and the dominions – which at that time had exactly the same decorations as the motherland – was that only the Victoria Cross and a Mention in Despatches could be awarded posthumously. This was grossly unfair. It was often the case that had a soldier lived after an action in which he had displayed great courage and leadership, he would have been awarded the DCM or MM, but because he died he was awarded nothing more than an MiD, which is not a decoration at all. Indeed, some men who were killed in an action were actually recommended for the VC, but when this was not approved they were awarded a posthumous MiD. This was outrageously unreasonable, but no steps were taken to correct the anomaly for another sixty years.

The French system was more just. The authorities awarded a posthumous Croix de Guerre to every soldier killed in action and it was passed to his next of kin. The French attitude was that a soldier who gave his life could hardly have been more heroic.

In all the armies listed in this section, other decorations and gradations of award were introduced in later years, especially in the German Army during 1939–45. Also, in the British Army more decorations became available for posthumous award. Australia, New Zealand and Canada introduced their own decorations for gallantry, while retaining the VC as the preeminent award for military courage.

BRITISH DECORATIONS

VICTORIA CROSS

Instituted in 1856, the decoration consists of a bronze cross pattée, 1½ in across with raised edges. On the back of the clasp is engraved the name, rank and regiment (or ship) of the recipient. Originally the ribbon was blue for the navy and crimson for the army but crimson was adopted during the First World War for the navy, army and air force.

Made initially from the bronze of captured guns, the VC is worth only a few pence intrinsically but is priceless in every other way. It is the most highly coveted decoration for any fighting man to obtain and it takes precedence over all other decorations and distinctions.

In the years 1914–18, 291 VCs were awarded to British personnel who survived the action for which they were decorated and 124 were awarded posthumously. Two men were awarded the VC twice: they were Captain A. Martin Leake of the RAMC and Captain N.G. Chevasse, also of the RAMC. Martin Leake had won his first VC in the Boer War, his second in 1914. He survived the war. Captain Chevasse first won the VC in 1916 and again in 1917, when he was killed.

The AIF was awarded sixty-three VCs, of which fourteen were posthumous; the CEF sixty-two VCs, of which twenty-two were posthumous; the NZEF twelve VCs,

British decorations. Left to right: top, CMG, DSC, MC, CB; middle, VC, DSO; bottom, DCM, MM, MSM, CGM.

of which three were posthumous; the SAEF four VCs; and the Indian Army eighteen VCs, including six posthumous.

DISTINGUISHED SERVICE ORDER

This Order was established in 1866 for meritorious or distinguished service in war. To qualify during 1914–18 a serviceman had to be a commissioned officer whose name had been specially mentioned in despatches for 'distin-guished service under fire or under conditions equivalent to service in actual combat with the enemy'.

The decoration was awarded generally to officers of lieutenant-colonel or above but many majors received it, as did even more junior officers. A subaltern who received it must have shown exceptional qualities.

THE MILITARY CROSS

An army decoration, the MC, a silver cross, was instituted on 31 December 1914 when the authorities realized that they needed some way of rewarding captains, lieutenants and warrant officers for outstanding bravery and leadership in action.

Not until 1931 could majors qualify for the MC. Because the Distinguished Flying Cross was not established until December 1918, many RFC/RAF officers were awarded the MC during the war.

DISTINGUISHED CONDUCT MEDAL

The DCM was introduced in 1854 to replace the Meritorious Service Medal for gallantry in action. On the obverse appears 'For Distinguished Conduct in the Field'. During the First World War it was awarded to NCOs and men.

THE MILITARY MEDAL

Sadly, the MM was not instituted until March 1916, by which time many brave acts had gone unrewarded for lack of an appropriate award. On its obverse appears 'For Bravery in the Field'. It is awarded to warrant officers, NCOs and men, and about forty-three thousand of them, throughout the British Empire Forces, were so decorated. Only one soldier won the MM four times – Private Bill Corey, a stretcher-bearer serving with the AIF.

MENTION IN DESPATCHES

An 'MiD' is not a decoration, but a soldier singled out for 'a mention' received a certificate to that effect. During the war an emblem of bronze oak leaves denoted a Mention in Despatches and was worn on the ribbon of the Victory Medal. Cynical soldiers said that an MiD was 'a failed MM'.

FRENCH DECORATIONS

LÉGION D'HONNEUR

The Légion d'Honneur was instituted by Napoleon I in 1802 as a way of rewarding distinguished military and civil service. The Order is divided into five grades: Grands Croix, Grands Officiers, Commandeurs, Officiers and Chevaliers. The award is the premier order of the nation and at the time of the First World War was only conferred for gallantry in action or for twenty years' distinguished military or civil service during peace.

French decorations, shown in *L'Illustration*, 1917, include, top row, left to right: Légion d'Honneur, Medaille Militaire, Croix de Guerre with palm.

'Valeur et Discipline'. An attractive decoration, the Medaille Militaire consists of a circular medal surmounted by a trophy of arms made up of crossed cannons, a cuirass, anchor, swords and muskets.

CROIX DE GUERRE

Like the British, the French Army realized after the first few months of the war that much heroism was passing unrewarded. The result was the Croix de Guerre, instituted on 8 April 1915. It was open to soldiers and sailors of all ranks, and to officers and men of Allied armies mentioned in a despatch from an officer commanding an army, corps, division, brigade or regiment. Emblems on the ribbon indicate the various classes of despatch for which the recipient was rewarded. Army Despatch – small bronze laurel branch; Corps Despatch – silver gilt star; Divisional Despatch – silver star; Brigade, Regimental or similar unit despatch – bronze star. Every mention was represented by its emblem, so that a man could wear the Cross with, for instance, the silver gilt and bronze palm. Many British soldiers were under the impression that an emblem made the Croix more important than one without an emblem; in fact, there was no such thing as an unadorned Croix de Guerre.

When given for war service it carried with it the automatic award of the Croix de Guerre with palm.

MEDAILLE MILITAIRE

Established in 1852, this is roughly the equivalent of the British DCM, but was awarded only to generals in command of armies and to NCOs who especially distinguished themselves in war. The centre of the reverse bears the words

BELGIAN DECORATIONS

The Belgian authorities were inspired by the French to introduce, in 1915, an award for courage in battle or for long service at the front. The bronze cross carries circular bronze or silver emblems on the ribbon bearing the Belgian lion, or palm to indicate further mentions. Unlike the French Croix de Guerre, the Belgian cross could be awarded without an embellishment on the ribbon.

YSER MEDAL
To mark the distinction of having taken part in the battles along the Yser river between 17 October and 31 October 1914, the Belgian government awarded a medal with the word Yser on the reverse. It hung from a medallion also bearing the word Yser. It is sometimes seen with four arms extended, making it into a cross, but this was not introduced until 1934.

UNITED STATES DECORATIONS

THE MEDAL OF HONOR
First introduced in 1861, the Medal of Honor is the supreme award of the United States and is awarded to officers and enlisted men for bravery in action involving actual conflict with the enemy and then only to those who distinguish themselves in some oustanding way – by their duty 'without detriment to the mission'. It was awarded only after stringent investigation as to the worthiness of any proposed recipient.

THE DISTINGUISHED SERVICE CROSS (ARMY)
This was very much inspired by the First World War and established in January 1918. It was for individual service personnel in the army who distinguished themselves by extraordinary heroism against an armed enemy under circumstances which did not justify the award of the Medal of Honor.

A recipient of the Cross who again distinguished himself wore an oak leaf cluster on the ribbon.

DISTINGUISHED SERVICE MEDAL (ARMY)
Instituted at the same time as the DSC in 1918, the DSM could be awarded to any person in the army for exceptionally meritorious service in the field or at any post of duty. The medal was awarded to a few officers in the British and Empire armies in 1918.

DISTINGUISHED FLYING CROSS
Not awarded until July 1926, the DFC retrospectively included 1917–18 service. The

bronze cross bears the design of a four-blade propeller superimposed on a chased square.

VICTORY MEDAL 1917–19

This medal, though *not* a decoration, is worth mentioning as the most interesting of 'Victory Medals' awarded by all the participating Allied nations. It was granted to all members of the US Army, Navy and Marine Corps, whether they served overseas or not, but the clasps that could be awarded with it made it militarily and historically valuable. These were the possible clasps: Cambrai, Somme Defensive, Lys, Aisne, Montdidier–Noyon, Champagne–Marne, Aisne–Marne, Somme Offensive, Oise–Aisne, Ypres–Lys, St Mihiel, Meuse–Argonne, Vittorio–Veneto. All of these were major operations. There also the clasp Defensive Sector, which was not. Five service clasps were also awarded – France, Italy, Siberia, Russia and England – but persons entitled to battle clasps did not wear the service clasps.

Some people may consider that these clasps overstressed the United States Army's role in the war but I believe that they were justified. The great shame was that Britain and its dominions did not award comparable clasps to their troops.

GERMAN DECORATIONS

POUR LE MÈRITE

In the First World War the Order of the Pour le Mèrite was the highest German reward for individual gallantry in action. After the defeat of Germany in 1918 it was never again awarded. The decoration was a Maltese cross in blue enamel, edged with gold and with four golden eagles between the limbs. On the upper arm of the cross was the letter F in gold surmounted by a crown and on the other three arms Pour le Mèrite. German fliers knew the Pour le Mèrite as the Blue Max.

THE IRON CROSS

Frederick William III introduced the Iron Cross in 1813. It was revived for the conflict of 1914–18 and lavishly distributed – 219,300 first class and 5,500,000 second class. Some authorities say that these numbers were for the entire period 1813–1918, but German sources indicate otherwise.

The simple decoration consisted of a cross pattée in black iron edged with silver, with a spray of oak leaves in the centre. The crown and royal cypher adorn the upper limb and the dates 1813, 1870 or 1914 are on the lower limb. The cross of the first class was pinned to the tunic, just like many Orders. The second-class decoration was worn on the breast from a black ribbon with white stripes. Various other grades of the Iron Cross were instituted by the Nazis for the Second World War.

A German war loans poster, showing a German soldier in uniform and gas mask. At bottom right can be seen the handles of grenades.

THE CROSS OF HONOUR

President Hindenburg retrospectively established this decoration in 1934 'to the memory of the imperishable deeds of the German people . . . for all participants as well as for widows and parents of those who fell or died of wounds or as prisoners of war or were reported missing and have not since been traced'. It was a bronze cross, again made of iron, with two swords passing through it and with the dates 1914–18 on the obverse. Crosses of Honour had to be applied for but even so millions of people did apply, throwing the German bureaucratic machine into chaos as every claim had to be investigated and reported on. One successful applicant was Adolf Hitler, a genuine front-line soldier, who had also been awarded the Iron Cross.

MEDALS RELEVANT TO WESTERN FRONT SERVICE

1914 STAR

Actually a campaign star and known incorrectly as the Mons Star, this star covered all service personnel who had served with a unit in France or Belgium between 5 August 1914 and 22–23 November 1914. On 19 October 1919 a bar was issued to those already awarded the 1914 Star who 'actually served under fire of the enemy' in France or Belgium between these dates. Thus, there are two types of 1914 Star, with and without the bar. Apart from a slight difference in the medal itself there is nothing to differentiate between an officer or man who received the 1914 Star without bar or the later authorized 1914–15 Star.

1914–15 STAR

Approved in 1918, this star is almost identical to the 1914 Star. The difference is that the date 1914–15 appears on the centre scroll and the words 'Aug' and 'Nov' are omitted from the smaller scrolls. In the army the star was awarded to all personnel, including nursing sisters, who served on the establishment of a unit in a theatre of war. Those people who already had the 1914 Star were ineligible for the 1914–15 Star.

BRITISH WAR MEDAL 1914–20

Awarded in 1920, this silver medal was in recognition of service. On the design the male figure rather than the traditional female figure was chosen because men had borne the brunt of the fighting. St George on horseback tramples underfoot the eagle shield of the Central Powers and a skull and crossbones, the symbols of death. A total of 5,670,170 War Medals were issued.

VICTORY MEDAL

This bronze medal struck in 1919 went to large numbers of personnel of whatever rank and in all the dominions. Members of women's organizations 'who

Pip, Squeak and Wilfred, the service medals of the First World War. From the left: 1914—15 Star, War Medal, Victory Medal. These medals belonged to Private, later Lieutenant, I.M. Ibbotson, AIF.

The reverse of Pip, Squeak and Wilfred, here named from the right.

177

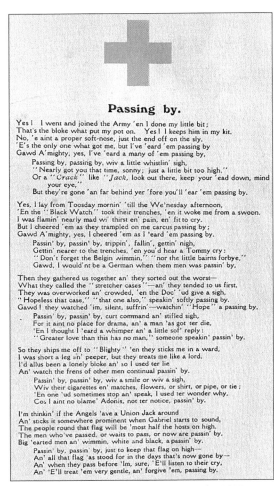

Passing by.

Yes! I went and joined the Army 'en I done my little bit;
That's the bloke what put my pot on. Yes! I keeps him in my kit.
No, 'e aint a proper soft-nose, just the end off on the sly.
'E's the only one what got me, but I've 'eard 'em passing by,
Gawd A'mighty, yes, I've 'eard a many of 'em passing by,

 Passing by, passing by, wiv a little whistlin' sigh,
 "Nearly got you that time, sonny; just a little bit too high."
 Or a "Crack" like "Jack, look out there, keep your 'ead down, mind
  your eye,"
 But they're gone 'an far behind yer 'fore you'll 'ear 'em passing by.

Yes, I lay from Toosday mornin' 'till the We'nesday afternoon,
'En the "Black Watch" took their trenches, 'en it woke me from a swoon.
I was flamin' nearly mad wi' thirst en' pain, en' fit to cry.
But I cheered 'em as they trampled on me carcus passing by;
Gawd A'mighty, yes, I cheered 'em as I 'eard 'em passing by.

 Passin' by, passin' by, trippin', fallin', gettin' nigh,
 Gettin' nearer to the trenches, 'en you'd hear a Tommy cry:
 "Don't forget the Belgin wimmin," "nor the little bairns forbye,"
 Gawd, I would'nt be a German when them men was passin' by,

Then they gathered us together an' they sorted out the worst—
What they called the "stretcher cases"—an' they tended to us first.
They was overworked an' crowded, 'en the Doc' 'ud give a sigh,
"Hopeless that case," "that one also," speakin' softly passing by.
Gawd! they watched 'im, silent, suffrin'—watchin' "Hope" a passing by,

 Passin' by, passin' by, curt command an' stifled sigh,
 For it aint no place for drama, an' a man 'as got ter die,
 'En I thought I 'eard a whimper an' a little sof' reply:
 "Greater love than this has no man," someone speakin' passin' by.

So they ships me off to "Blighty" 'en they sticks me in a ward,
I was short a leg an' peeper, but they treats me like a lord.
I'd allus been a lonely bloke an' so I used ter lie
An' watch the frens of other men continual passin' by.

 Passin' by, passin' by, wiv a smile or wiv a sigh,
 Wiv their cigarettes an' matches, flowers, or shirt, or pipe, or tie;
 'En one 'ud sometimes stop an' speak, I used ter wonder why,
 Cos I aint no 'blame' Adonis, not ter notice, passin' by.

I'm thinkin' if the Angels 'ave a Union Jack around
An' sticks it somewhere prominent when Gabriel starts to sound,
The people round that flag will be 'most half the hosts on high.
The men who've passed, or waits to pass, or now are passin' by,
Big 'earted men an' wimmin, white and black, a passin' by.

 Passin' by, passin' by, just to keep that flag on high—
 An' all that flag 'as stood for in the days that's now gone by—
 An' when they pass before 'Im, sure, 'E'll listen to their cry,
 An' 'E'll treat 'em very gentle, an' forgive 'em, passing by.

This poem by a wounded soldier, written in November 1915, says much about the troops' attitudes at the time. The poem, printed on a card, with a Red Cross at the top, was sold to raise funds for soldiers' comforts.

1918–1933

Did I dream then that passion flaming white,
 Sorrow and every soul-searched, tragic day,
The slim years passing, would no more be
  bright;
Could I foresee the Sacrifice of Right
 Flouted; and know forgetting is our way?

Where are the comradeships we swore to keep,
 Sharing the jagged fragments of a butt
Through the harsh silence of a world asleep,
But strangely watchful; were they then too
  cheap
 Or far too precious for the daily rut?

Those who went on when we have but come
  back.
 Yes, I remember here and there a name,
Vaguely, and vagrant incidents that track
Into my mind; but all the rest is black
 As that dead fire that yesterday was flame.

Those are forgotten save in odd regard,
 Estaminets, "Five nines" and that "BB."
At Abbeville, so proud to be so hard,
Yet linger; and though retrospect has marred
 Her splendors, still I muse about Marie.

         – J.K.M.

A later poem by 'J.K.M.' remembering the First World War, published in a magazine of 1 November 1933.

had been enrolled under a direct contract of service with His Majesty's Imperial Forces' received the medal, as well as civil medical staff working in military hospitals. The small bronze oak leaf for a Mention in Despatches, and for any number of 'mentions', was worn on the ribbon of the Victory Medal. A vast number of people qualified for the medal – 5,125,403.

The 1914 or 1914–15 Star, the War Medal and the Victory Medal were the 'Pip', 'Squeak' and 'Wilfred' of soldier-speak.

CHAPTER NINE

PLACES OF SPECIAL INTEREST

Extending for a length of more than 460 miles and with a depth of several miles – up to 30 or 40 miles if 'rear areas' are included – the Western Front contains innumerable cities, towns and villages that were affected by the war. The Ypres Salient alone comprises about sixty settlements, while the area on which the first Battle of the Somme was fought – it was more accurately an offensive – contains more than two hundred towns and villages.

This gazetteer lists the most important of them on the basis of their degree of interest to visitors more than seventy-five years after the end of the war. Some places which were of major strategic or tactical importance in the period 1914–18, and which were ferociously fought over, today show little evidence of conflict.

My classification of one star to five stars indicates the level of interest *now* rather than the level of interest to generals during the war. In many cases the two are of equal importance, such as the Ypres Salient and the Verdun battlefield.

***** Several military cemeteries, memorials, plaques and musems. There is a lot to see.

**** Similar, but perhaps lacking a museum.

*** Interesting but probably has only one major feature of interest for pilgrims.

** Don't expect too much despite many mentions in official histories.

* Worth looking at in passing but the war has left little trace.

For descriptions in detail, refer to a guidebook.

ABBEVILLE, PICARDY
A headquarters town for the British front on the Somme, Abbeville was also a railhead distribution point and a hospital base. Cemetery. *

ABEELE
West of Poperinge, this hamlet on the French–Belgian border had an RFC/RAF airfield. Cemetery. *

ACHINCOURT, ARRAS
Part of the Arras battlefield and much shelled by the German guns. Cemetery. *

ACHIET LE GRAND AND ACHIET LE PETIT
Villages which were part of the First Somme battlefield. Cemeteries. *

AISNE, RIVER AND DEPARTMENT
A large area of France in which several great battles were fought, largely for control of the river crossings. * * *

ALBERT
British forward base for First Somme. The town, known as 'Bert' to the troops, figures largely in all accounts of the Somme and is the site of the basilica of the 'Leaning Virgin'. It is the ideal base for visiting the battlefields. Cemeteries, memorials, plaques, museum. * * * * *

ALTDORF
Scene of 1914–15 battles and a good base for touring Lorraine and the Vosges. * * *

AMIENS
This city was a great British and French supply and route centre and strategically important. The Battle of Amiens is the name given to the battles of 1918, fought well to the east, which saved the city

Frechencourt Communal Cemetery Extension, in a secluded garden between Amiens and Albert. Of the fifty-seven men buried here, forty-nine are Australian and all but one of them are artillerymen. Obscure little cemeteries such as this one are rarely visited.

from capture. The cathedral has plaques to Australians and New Zealanders. *****

ANCRE, RIVER
In part, this river skirting Albert was the front line at the onset of the British 1 July 1916 offensive. There was much fighting along the river. It is best seen at St Pierre Divion. Cemeteries. ****

APREMONT
Near St Mihiel. French and later American attacks were made from this town against the Germans in the rolling country beyond. ****

ARLEUX-EN-GOHELLE
Near Vimy Ridge. Scene of fierce fighting in 1915 and 1917. *

ARMENTIÈRES
This large town near Lille was held in turn by the Germans and Allies, for whom it was a symbol of the Western Front. It was finally recaptured by the French and British in September 1918. Several cemeteries. ****

ARRAS
Devastated by enemy shelling, Arras was close behind the lines until April 1917. Civilians and troops lived in caverns and tunnels under the city. Several cemeteries, notably the British Military Cemetery in Faubourg d'Amiens and the Arras Memorial to the Missing (35,928 names), many memorials and plaques. ******

ARTOIS
The undulating region south of French Flanders. The scene of costly British battles in 1915. Worth exploring. ****

AUBERS
This village on Aubers Ridge, south of Armentières, was the scene of abortive British attacks in 1914, 1915 and 1916. Cemeteries, memorials. ***

AUCHONVILLERS
North-east of Albert. A village on the British front of First Somme. Cemeteries. *

AVELUY WOOD
Near Albert, on the Ancre river. Much fighting took place in this forest in 1914–15 and again in 1916. Cemetery. ****

BAILLEUL
French–Belgian border. A British forward base and leave town from 14 October 1914. Shelled and damaged in July 1917. Shelled again and captured in April 1918. Recaptured on 30 August 1918. Large cemetery on the site of an RFC airfield. ****

BAPAUME
East of Albert. The Germans held this town until 1917. They then wrecked and fired it before withdrawing. Cemetery. ***

BAZENTIN-LE-PETIT AND BAZENTIN-LE-GRAND
East of Albert. These hamlets were places of heavy fighting during First Somme. Cemeteries. ****

BEAUCOURT
East of Albert. Scene of heavy fighting during First Somme. ***

BEAUMONT-HAMEL
The ruins of this village were the front line on 1 July 1918. The Newfoundland Regiment was wiped out in fields above the settlement. Site of several cemeteries, many memorials, and areas of the battlefield have been preserved. *****

BEAURAINS
Near Arras. An area of heavy fighting in 1917. Cemetery. *

BECOURT
Near Albert. Part of the start line for the 1 July offensive 1916. Cemeteries. **

BELFORT
The southern end of the Western Front trench line and a communications centre for the French. **

BELLEAU WOOD
Near Château-Thierry. Site of the US Aisne–Marne Cemetery. Chapel, observation platform. ***

BELLENGLISE
Part of the German defences on the St Quentin Canal. Australian memorial on the hill above the village. **

BELLEWARDE, YPRES SALIENT
Heavy fighting took place here, especially in the summer of 1917. Much of Bellewarde is now a zoo and amusement park. **

BELLICOURT
The Germans incorporated this town into their Hindenburg Line defences; it is above the underground St Quentin Canal. The AIF and AEF were involved in heavy and costly fighting here in September 1918. Cemetery. ***

BERNAFAY WOOD
East of Albert. A much fought-for wood in July 1916 and after. Cemetery on the edge of the wood. ***

BERTANGLES
Near Amiens. Site of several British and Australian corps and divisional HQs at the château. Also the site of Richthofen's burial in the churchyard on 22 April 1918. ****

BERTINCOURT
North-east of Bapaume. Scene of fighting in April 1917. *

BESELARE
East of Ypres. This village, in German hands until September 1918, anchored the left flank of the enemy hold on the Passchendaele–Beselare ridge. *

BETHUNE, FRENCH FLANDERS
A British HQ, billeting and supply town and rail centre. Cemetery. ***

The Liverpool Scottish during an action at Hooge in 1915. (IWM Q49750)

BOEZINGE, YPRES SALIENT

Site of the German gas attack on 22 April 1915. Patrol actions took place here and heavier fighting in summer 1917. Cemetery; the gas attack memorial. ***

BOIS GRENIER

Near Armentières. This village was part of the 'Nursery' where British and Empire troops were given early trench experience. Scene of fighting in April–July 1916. Cemeteries. ***

BOURLON WOOD

Near Cambrai. Site of a major Canadian victory in September 1918. Canadian memorial. *****

BRANDHOEK
Near Poperinge. A mere hamlet, Brandhoek was the site of field hospitals and several cemeteries, including the burial place of Noel Chevasse, a double VC winner. His headstone is the only one in the world with two VCs engraved upon it.[1] ***

BRIELEN
Near Ypres. A small village totally destroyed during the war. *

BRAY
Near Albert. On the steep northern bank of the Somme, Bray was at the junction of the British Third and Fifth Armies in March 1918. Captured by the AIF on 24–5 August 1918. Cemetery. **

BROODSEINDE, YPRES SALIENT
This village on the Passchendaele–Beselare Ridge was held by the Germans until it was captured by the AIF in October 1917.*

BUCQUOY
Near Arras. This village was behind German lines and was an administrative centre until pounded by British guns. Captured by the British in March 1917 and defended against the Germans

in their spring advance of 1918. Cemeteries. **

BULLECOURT
Near Arras. This small village gave its name to two battles fought by the AIF in April–May 1917. Cemeteries, museums, several AIF memorials. *****

BUS-LES-ARTOIS
British concentration area before the renewal of First Somme attack, 12 July 1916. *

BUTTE DE MONT FAUCON, VERDUN BATTLEFIELD
This hill fell to the AEF on 27 September 1918. American memorial, cemetery. *****

BUTTE DE VAUQUOIS, VERDUN BATTLEFIELD
French and Germans mined and countermined this hill. Today many craters and much barbed wire remain. Memorials. *****

BUTTE DE WARLENCOURT
Near Bapaume. An artificial mound, fortified and tunnelled by the Germans. It marks the end of the British First Somme Offensive. The German Army tactically withdrew in March 1917 but in March 1918 swept over the Butte and the entire 1916 battlefield. Finally, in August 1918, the British regained the Butte as the Germans pulled back for the last time. Cemetery, memorial. ****

[1] When Lieutenant Charles Upham of New Zealand dies his grave might well be similarly engraved. Both his VCs were won in the Middle East during the Second World War. Only three men have ever won the VC twice.

One of the most unusual memorials on the Western Front. An original digger hat was bronzed and attached to a stone above a plaque at the village of Bullecourt, east of Bapaume, where the AIF fought two battles in April and May 1917.

The Butte de Warlencourt, one of the most famous landmarks of the British and Empire section of the Western Front. The Battle of the Somme, 1916, came to an end here with the exhausted British unable to wrest the butte from the entrenched Germans.

BUZANCY
Near Soissons. Scene of fighting by the French and British in 1918. Cemetery, Scottish memorial. * * * *

CABARET ROUGE
North of Arras. Site of a village destroyed in French–German fighting in 1915. Cemetery, Indian memorial. * * *

CACHY
Near Villers Bretonneux. Scene of an AIF attack against the Germans, and of a gas attack by the Germans in April 1918. *

CAGNICOURT
Part of the Bullecourt battlefield (q.v.).

CAMBRAI
Captured by Germans in 1914, this village was HQ for Prince Rupprecht of Bavaria. It was mined and fired by the Germans as the British and Canadians approached in September 1918. Cemetery, memorials. * * * * *

CANTIGNY
Near Montdidier. This village was held by the German Eighteenth Army when captured by the American First Division on 28 May 1918, the first US engagement of the war. * *

CAPPY, SOMME
A village behind Allied lines until March

The artillery memorial at Cologne commemorates the gallantry of a young officer during the Battle of Cambrai. When his gun was put out of action, with all its crew dead, he tried to hold off the British tanks with grenades until he too was killed.

1918. The airfield then became one of Richthofen's bases. It was captured by the AIF in August 1918. *

CASSEL
West of Calais, this hill town was the HQ of various British and French commanders, including Foch, Haig and Plumer. Museum. ***

CAUDRY
Near Le Cateau. This town was captured by the Germans in 1914. The site of a larger battle in 1918, it was liberated on 10 October 1918. Memorial. ***

CERNY-EN-LAONNAIS
A crossroads village on the crest of Chemin-des-Dames ridge. Cemeteries, memorials. *****

CHAMBRECY
Near Reims. A village prominent in the defence of Reims. Italian cemetery and memorial garden, British cemetery. ***

CHAMERY
Near Reims. Site of the air crash of Quentin Roosevelt, son of President Theodore Roosevelt, on 14 July 1918. Memorial fountain in town square. ***

CHAMPAGNE
This region was fought over by the AEF in July 1918. Cemeteries. ***

CHÂTEAU ROUGE
Near Landrecies. Scene of the British

First Division's stands on 26 August 1914 and on 4 November 1918. Cemetery, memorial. ****

CHÂTEAU-THIERRY
Scene of part of First Marne on 9 September 1914, and site of the first AEF offensive in May–July 1918. Site of an immense memorial. ****

CHIPILLY
A First Somme village on the river bank. Memorial. **

COMBLES, SOMME
An important fortified village, surrounded by hills, in the German defence system of Somme. Cemetery. ***

COMPIÈGNE
The Armistice was signed on 11 November 1918 in a railway carriage in the forest of Compiègne. The original coach disappeared in Germany in the Second World War but a substitute is in its place. *****

CONTALMAISON
Near Albert. The British captured this village on 9 July 1916, early in First Somme.

COTE 304, VERDUN BATTLEFIELD
Nearly twenty thousand men died in this area. Memorial. ***

CORBIE, SOMME
A busy forward town during First Somme. **

COURCELETTE

Near Albert. This village, close to Pozières, was the site of a major Canadian attack in September 1916. Cemetery, memorial. * * *

CRAONNE

A town close to the 'California' position used by Napoleon in 1814, and prominent in 1914 and 1917. The British IX Corps was routed here on 27 May 1918. Cemeteries, French memorials, orientation table. * * *

DELVILLE WOOD

East of Albert. Site of much fighting during First Somme, notably the stand of the South African Brigade, 14–20 July 1916. Cemeteries, South African memorial, museum. * * * * *

DIKKEBUS (DICKEBUSH), YPRES

A British concentration point, gun position and dumps area. Cemeteries. * * *

DIXMUIDE

North of Ypres. Dixmuide, on the River Yser, became famous for its 'Trench of Death' along the river bank. The Belgians, who held the line on that side of the river, with the Germans on the other bank, reconstructed the trench and dugouts and they can be visited. * * * *

DOUAUMONT, VERDUN

A major fort in the city's defences. Cemetery, Ossuary of Douaumont, Jewish memorial. * * * * *

DOULLENS

Foch's HQ, then a BEF base and concentration area. Foch was appointed Supreme Allied Commander here on 26 March 1918. Cemetery, remembrance chamber in Hôtel de Ville. * * *

ELVERDINGE

Near Ypres. The centre of many British camps, training areas, dumps and hospitals. It was heavily shelled. *

ERVILLERS

Near Bapaume. A German garrison village until March 1917. It was the scene of heavy fighting in March 1918 as British troops tried to block the German advance. *

ÉTAPLES

Near Boulogne. One of the largest BEF centres for training depots, hospitals and dumps. Large cemetery. * * *

FERE-EN-TARDENOIS

British GHQ between 12 September and 8 October 1914. It was captured by Germans in May 1918. *

FESTUBERT, FRENCH FLANDERS

Site of battles in October 1914 and May 1916. In April 1918 the defence of Festubert checked the German advance in the Battle of the Lys. British blockhouse and bunker. *

FEUCHY
Near Arras. Scene of fighting during the British advance of April 1917. Memorial. **

FLERS
East of Albert. Site of the first British tank attack, September 1916, and much other fighting. Memorial. **

FLESQUIÈRES
Near Cambrai. Site of a major part of the Battle of Cambrai on 20 November 1917. Cemetery. *

FLEURBAIX, FRENCH FLANDERS
Scene of much fighting in 1916 and 1918. The Battle of Fromelles (q.v.) was first known as the Battle of Fleurbaix. Cemeteries. *

FLEURY, VERDUN
One of nine villages obliterated by shell-fire during the 1916 battles. Site of the magnificent Memorial de Verdun. Museum. *****

FORT DE LA POMPELLE
Near Reims. A strongpoint in Reims' defences. Museum. ***

FREZENBERG, YPRES SALIENT
This village gives its name to a ridge vital in 1915 and 1917. Batteries positioned here stopped the German advance of 24 April 1915. *

FRICOURT
Near Albert. A German fortress village and site of mine warfare. British and German cemeteries, memorial. ***

FROMELLES, FRENCH FLANDERS
Site of the Battle of Fromelles on 19–20 July 1916, when the AIF Fifth Division lost 5,333 men. Cemeteries, including VC Corner Australian Cemetery, memorials, museum. *****

GAVRELLE
Near Arras. Scene of an attack by the Royal Naval Division on 23 April 1917 and its subsequent defence of the town. It was captured by the Germans in March 1918 and recaptured on 27 August 1918. Memorial. *

GHELUVELT, YPRES SALIENT
A village on the Menin Road, captured by the Germans in October 1914 but recaptured. Memorials. **

GINCHY
East of Albert. A village in the German defence line before First Somme. It changed hands three times in the fighting of July 1916. ***

GIVENCHY
North of Arras. This small village was the scene of frequent fighting for much of the war. Cemetery. *

GOMIECOURT
Near Bapaume. The scene of fighting in August 1918, when the British Third Division captured it with many prisoners. *

GOMMECOURT
North of Albert. The edge of this village was part of the British Third Army Front on 1 July 1916 but it did not fall until February 1917. Cemetery. *

GUEUDECOURT
East of Albert. Centre of many actions during 1916, especially September 1916. Newfoundland memorial. ***

GUILLEMONT
East of Albert. Site of intense fighting in August and September 1916. Panoramic views, cemeteries, memorials. ***

HAMEL
Near Villers Bretonneux. See Le Hamel.

HANGARD WOOD
Near Villers Bretonneux. Scene of heavy fighting by the AIF in April 1918. Cemetery. ***

HARELBEKE, FLANDERS
Scene of fighting in September 1918. Newfoundland Regiment memorial. *

HAVRINCOURT
Near Cambrai. A fortified village and wood from which the Germans could not be dislodged. It lay on the edge of the Battle of Cambrai in November 1917. Cemetery, memorial, bunkers. **

HAZEBROUCK, FRENCH FLANDERS
BEF and AIF billeting, administrative and railway town. Cemetery. **

HÉBUTERNE
North of Albert. A British fortified village and start-point for First Somme on 1 July 1916. The scene of AIF actions, March–April 1918. Cemetery. *

HERMIES
Between Bapaume and Cambrai. A village noted for AIF actions in 1917. Cemetery. *

LA BOISELLE
East of Albert. This village was precisely on the front line when the British Somme Offensive began on 1 July 1916. Lochnagar Crater was created by one of the mines blown by the British and even today it measures 300 ft across by 90 ft deep. It is one of the great sights of the Western Front and has become a shrine. La Boiselle has other British memorials. *****

LE HAMEL
See Hamel.

LENS
Near Bethune. German fortified town which became the centre of fighting in tunnels and on slagheaps. The Canadians captured part of the sector in August 1917 and there were further British attacks in September 1917 and January 1918. The ruins were captured on 2 October 1918. Cemetery. *

LE QUESNOY
Near Valenciennes. After the BEF retreat of

Lochnagar crater near the village of La Boiselle. It was created by 27 tons of ammonal on 1 July 1916, the first day of the Battle of the Somme. From the air these fields still show the chalk which was brought to the surface by mining, shelling and trench-digging. The road through La Boiselle goes to Pozières, 2 km away. (*After the Battle* magazine)

August 1914 the Germans fortified the place, which became a garrison town. On 5 November 1918 men of the NZEF scaled the ramparts and captured the garrison. Unusual New Zealand memorial. * * *

LE SARS
Near Bapaume. Centre of much fighting in 1916 and the limit of the British advance in First Somme. *

LESBOEUFS
East of Albert. A Somme village destroyed in the fighting of First Somme. Cemetery,

Guards memorial. *

LES EPARGES, ARGONNE
Centre of ferocious French–German conflict, with much mining. Cemeteries, several French memorials, craters. * * *

LOCRE
Near Bailleul. A village destroyed in the battles for Mont Kemmel. Cemetery, memorial plaques. * * *

LONGUEVAL
East of Albert. This village was destroyed

Funeral of a private of the 2nd Scots Guards. Battlefield burials were much more hurried and basic than this one. (IWM Q57393)

in the fierce fighting of July 1916. Cemeteries, New Zealand memorial. See Delville Wood. **

LOOS
Near Bethune. Site of a major battle, 25 September–13 October 1915, with heavy BEF casualties. This was the first use of poison gas by the British. Cemetery, Loos Memorial to the Missing of the Loos, Lys, Estaires and Bethune fronts (20,589 names).**

'LOST BATTALION' RAVINE
Near Apremont (q.v.), Argonne. An AEF battalion was cut off between 2 and 7 October 1918 and became legendary for its heroism. There is a directional marker on the D442. **

LOUVERVAL
Between Bapaume and Cambrai. This hamlet was destroyed in the fighting of March 1917. Cemetery, Cambrai memorial. **

MAILLY MAILLET
North of Albert. Just behind the British lines before 1 July 1916, this village was heavily shelled and had many tunnels. A church with medieval façade survived the bombardments. ***

MAMETZ
Near Albert. The Germans fortified Mametz Wood so that on 1 July 1916 the British forces had to fight for it trench by trench. Cemeteries nearby, Welsh memorial. ***

MARFAUX

Near Reims. In June–July 1918 this village was the scene of severe fighting. Cemetery, Memorial to the New Zealand Missing. ***

MASNIÈRES

Near Cambrai. The BEF crossed a bridge over the St Quentin Canal at Masnières during the Battle of Cambrai and there was fighting in the town. Newfoundland Regiment's Caribou Memorial. **

MESSINES (MESEN)

Near Ypres. Target of the British attack of 7 June 1917, Messines was captured by the New Zealand Division with the AIF Third and Fourth divisions. Cemeteries: New Zealand Memorial to the Missing, NZ Memorial Park, London Scottish memorial, museum. *****

METEREN

Near Bailleul. Saved from the German advance in 1914, Meteren was overrun in March 1918 but recaptured by Scottish troops on 9 July. They lost it and it was recaptured by the AIF First Division on 19 July. Cemetery. *

MONT CASSEL

Briefly the HQ of Sir John French in October 1914, then of General Foch and for two years of General Plumer. Memorials, museum, plaques, orientation tables and a panoramic view over the battlefields of Messines, the Yser and Ypres.***

A 2nd Division digger stands astride his plinth on Mont St Quentin, captured by the AIF in a great feat of arms in September 1918. This is the finest AIF memorial on the Western Front.

MONT ST ELOI

Near Arras. In 1915 the French used the ruined towers of the Augustinian abbey as an observation post. The RFC had an airfield in the village. **

MONT ST QUENTIN

Near Peronne. Site of a famous AIF victory on 31 August 1918; marked by a splendid digger memorial. ****

MONTREUIL

Near Étaples, east of Boulogne. Site of British GHQ and its five thousand staff between March 1916 and April 1919.

Haig lived in the nearby Château de Beaurepaire. Memorials. ***

MOUQUET FARM
Pozières, near Albert. British, AIF and CEF objective and scene of ferocious battles, July–September 1916. The fortified farm was destroyed but later rebuilt. ***

MORT HOMME, VERDUN.
Scene of heavy fighting and much tunnelling in the great battle of 1916. Memorial. ***

NERY
South of Compiègne. Site of an artillery action on 1 September 1914 when L Battery RHA won three VCs in a gallant action. **

NEUVE CHAPELLE
North of La Bassée. Scene of much fighting. The village was captured by the Germans on 27 October 1914 and was retaken by the Indian Corps. Following the Allied withdrawal, British and Indian troops attacked Neuve Chapelle in force on 10 March 1915 and suffered heavy casualties. Cemetery, Indian memorial. ***

NEUVILLE ST VAAST, VIMY RIDGE
Scene of much fighting, 1915–17. Memorials, British, French and German (44,000 graves). Cemeteries, museum. ****

NIEWPOORT
North-west end of the front line and near the lockgates which were opened to flood the region and block the Germans' advance. Cemetery, British Memorial to the Missing, Belgian Memorial to King Albert. ****

NIMY, MONS
Scene of a battle in August 1914 at the lock and railway bridge. Plaques. ***

NOTRE DAME DE LORETTE
North of Arras. Site of the French National Memorial and Cemetery to commemorate the bloody fighting for the ridge on which they stand. Cemetery with 20,000 burials and an additional 21,000 in the ossuary. Museum. *****

ORS
Near Landrecies. Much fighting took place in this village on the Sambre Canal. Cemeteries – Wilfred Owen, KIA 4 November 1918, is buried in Ors Communal Cemetery. Memorial. ***

ORVILLERS
Near Albert. The Germans held out in fortifications between 1 and 14 July 1916 during First Somme. Cemetery. ***

PASSCHENDAELE (PASSENDALE), YPRES SALIENT
Passchendaele Ridge was the scene of some of the most costly battles of the war, notably July–November 1917. Site of Tyne Cot British Cemetery and Memorial to the Missing, British, Canadian and Belgian memorials. *****

PERONNE, SOMME

The Germans fortified this town on the river and destroyed it when retreating in March 1917. They recaptured and fortified it in March–April 1918 and it was captured by the AIF on 2 September 1918. Great museum, cemetery, memorials. * * * *

PLOEGSTEERT (PLUGSTREET), YPRES SALIENT

The village and wood were held by British and Empire troops for much of the war, as the position anchored the southern side of the salient. Cemeteries, British Memorial to the Missing. * * *

POLYGON WOOD, NEAR ZONNEBEKE, YPRES SALIENT

Scene of heavy fighting in British attempts to capture the Broodseinde–Beselare Ridge. Cemetery, AIF and NZEF memorials. * * * *

POPERINGE, BELGIAN FLANDERS

Behind Ypres, Poperinge was a railway point, hospital bath town and a short-leave town. Cemeteries, Talbot House (Toc H). * * * * *

POZIÈRES

Near Albert. The Germans fortified the ruins of this village and its ridge and the British, AIF and CEF made several costly attempts to capture it. Cemetery, British Memorial to the Missing of the Fifth Army in 1918, Tank Corps Memorial, two AIF memorials, plaque. * * * * *

Part of the immense British cemetery of Lijssenthoek, near Poperinge. Nearly 12,000 soldiers of the British Empire armies are buried here.

RAMSKAPELLE

North of Ypres. Site of Belgian resistance to the Germans. Memorial. *

REIMS

The German Army briefly occupied Reims before the French retook it. German guns then mercilessly shelled the city until 1918 and set fire to the cathedral. The French defended the ruins from a ring of forts, one of which, Fort de la Pompelle, is a war museum. * * * *

ROUEN

This city, to the immediate rear of the Western Front, was the site of several military hospitals, camps, supply units such as field bakeries, and workshops. It has one of the largest military cemeteries in France, St Sever, with 7,000 graves. * * *

SAILLY LE SEC, SOMME

A river hamlet around which much fighting occurred in 1916 and again in 1918. Cemeteries, Australian memorial. * * *

SPANBROEKMOLEN, YPRES

Near Wytschaete. Site of one of the nineteen great mines blown up under the German trenches on 7 June 1917. The vast crater became a lake, now known as the 'Pool of Peace'. * * *

ST JULIEN (ST JULIAAN), YPRES SALIENT

The Germans captured the position after their gas attack on 2 April 1915 and fortified it with blockhouses. The British and Empire troops attacked in July 1917 and after extremely heavy loss they captured the sector on 3 August. Cemeteries, Canadian memorial, rebuilt *Totenmuhle* (German observation mill). * * * *

STE MENEHOULD, ARGONNE SECTOR

The Germans captured the French fortress town in September 1914 and were driven out after much fighting. Until 1918 Ste Menehould was a French HQ and starting point for offensives. Cemeteries, memorials. * * *

ST MIHIEL, ARGONNE FRONT

Famous as the St Mihiel Salient, the AEF First Army attacked and reduced the salient in September 1918, one of the war's great triumphs. American cemetery and memorial. * * *

ST OMER

Near Calais. The RFC/RAF HQ town from January 1917 to November 1918; BEF GHQ October 1914–April 1916. Bombed by enemy aircraft and shelled by artillery in 1918. *

ST QUENTIN

Famous during the early days of the Western Front. St Quentin was the site of BEF HQ for 25/26 August 1914. The demoralized BEF retreated to the squares of St Quentin until forced out by the onrushing Germans. In March 1918 the Germans launched much of their spring offensive from St Quentin and they held it until 1 October 1918. Cemeteries, French memorial. * * *

SOISSONS

A key city in Western Front fighting. The Germans withdrew from Soissons on 12 September 1914, blew all the Aisne bridges and the Battle of the Aisne began next day. The BEF crossing of the Aisne, by boat, pontoon and raft, was one of the great feats of the war. The British advance was blocked along the Chemin-des-Dames sector. The French repulsed German attacks on Soissons in 1915 and 1917 but the enemy captured it in May

1918. On 2 August the French took it back. Cemeteries, British Soissons Memorial to the Missing (3,987 names). * * * *

SOUAIN–PERTHES–LES HURLUS, ARGONNE SECTOR
Centre of much fighting throughout the war. French and German cemeteries. * *

THIEPVAL
Near Albert. A ridge hamlet turned by the Germans into an immense fortress, much of it below ground. During First Somme the British struggled from 1 July to 28 September 1916 to capture it. The losses were appalling. Several cemeteries and several memorials, notably the Memorial to the Missing (73,412 names for 1916–17) and Ulster Division memorial. * * * * *

VAUQUOIS
See Butte de Vauquois.

VERDUN
The greatest French place of battle on the Western Front. The city narrowly escaped capture in 1914 and the main battle began in February 1916 with a tremendous German artillery and infantry attack. That year about 500,000 men became casualties. The main cemetery and memorial is at Douaumont. Numerous other memorials, notably the avenue of giant statues of marshals and generals of France. The main museum is at the Citadel fortress, much of it underground. * * * * *

VILLERS BRETONNEUX
Attacked and occupied by the Germans in April 1918. Villers Bretonneux was defended mainly by the AIF and it was the Australians who recaptured the town on 25 April. The place was the centre of conflict for four months and from here, on 8 August, the AIF began its part in the great and final Allied advance. Several cemeteries, notably the British Military Cemetery in front of the Australian National Memorial; site of the annual Anzac Day ceremonies on 25 April. Several French and Australian memorials, notably at the local school. * * * * *

VIMY RIDGE
North of Arras. In 1915 the French lost heavily in attempts to regain this strategic ridge. Plans to retake it began in 1916 with lengthy and cavernous tunnels dug under the ridge. Many mines were also blown by both sides. From this elaborate complex the Battle of Vimy began on 9 April 1917 and the CEF captured the ridge. Several cemeteries and memorials, notably the Canadian National Memorial. In addition, lengths of the trenches have been reconstructed and the tunnels are open for guided visits. The battlefield is covered with craters and shell-holes. * * * * *

VIS-EN-ARTOIS
East of Arras. Centre of a hotly contested sector in April 1917, in March 1918 during the German onslaught, and in August 1918. Cemeteries, notably Vis-en-

Graves of Australian soldier-tunnellers in Hersin Communal Cemetery, northern France. They died during fighting underground, beneath the slagheaps in the background.

Wounded in close-quarter fighting against jackbooted German soldiers, a French soldier is unable to finish a letter before his death. A painting by

Artois Cemetery and Memorial to the Missing of the 1918 advance (9,903 names). See also two memorials at nearby Monchy le Preux. *****

YPRES (IEPER)
This town gives its name to the Ypres Salient, where there was fighting throughout the war. There are fifty-five British cemeteries, together with French, Belgian and German cemeteries, within the salient. Many memorials, plaques, museums and commemorative sites, notably the Menin Gate, part of which is the British Memorial to the Missing (55,000 names between 1914 and August 1917); Cloth Hall war museum; St George's Memorial Church; Hill 60

Menin Gate, set into the ramparts of the ancient town of Ypres (now Ieper). The walls inside and outside are covered with the names of nearly 55,000 British and Empire soldiers who were killed in Belgium and have no known grave.

memorials and museum; Sanctuary Wood trenches and museum; Hooge Crater museum. *****

ZANDVOORDE, YPRES SALIENT

The Household Cavalry charged the Germans here on 26 October 1914, First Ypres. In a meadow the victorious Germans found two British cavalry squadrons dead or dying. Cemeteries, memorials, German bunker. ***

ZEEBRUGGE

Site of the Royal Navy's dramatic raid on St George's Day 1918 in an attempt to block German submarine access to the Bruges Canal. Memorial to the Missing, plaques; museum to be re-established. ***

CHAPTER TEN

THE COMMONWEALTH WAR GRAVES COMMISSION

The Commonwealth War Graves Commission – until 1960 the Imperial War Graves Commission – is so well established and so pre-eminently important wherever British, Canadian, Australian, New Zealand, South African, Indian and Pakistani troops have served that it is difficult to believe that it began virtually by chance.

In 1914 a British Red Cross ambulance unit under Fabian Ware was sent to France, mainly to work with the French Army. Ware visited Bethune cemetery with a Red Cross friend, Dr Stewart, who commented that the British wooden crosses were adequate as markers but lamented that the soldiers' names were not registered. Ware's small unit could do this work, Stewart said.

Ware went diligently to work. He and his men located and registered thousands of British Empire graves, and as the work became all-consuming the medical side of the unit's work was abandoned. In March 1915 it became the Graves Registration Commission and Ware was made a major, reporting to the adjutant-general.

A farsighted man, Ware negotiated with the French government to ensure that the British cemeteries would be permanent. In December 1915 the French promulgated a law, the results of which are evident in the notice displayed in all the cemeteries, that the land is a gift in perpetuity in recognition of the sacrifice of the Allied soldiers. In fact, the French government bought the land from the private owners. The Belgian government made similar arrangements and gave cemetery land to the British.

As part of the British Army, Ware's commission became the Directorate of Graves Registration and Enquiries early in 1916. Ware, now a colonel, established his HQ in London in order to centralize the enormous amount of work caused by the heavy casualties. He had already put in hand the photographing of graves to meet the needs of relatives, and now he persuaded the army to do away with the old metal identity tag and glazed linen tunic identity label and issue double identity discs of compressed fibre. One would stay with the body when buried, the other would be kept for record purposes.

During 1916 the Royal Botanic Gardens at Kew sent plants and seeds for

At the entrance to French military cemeteries a weatherproof noticeboard gives details of French battlefields and memorials in the district.

the new cemeteries, though the cost was borne by the Red Cross. Nurseries were set up at this time as well. Much to the surprise of officials, many soldiers used the cemeteries as places for a quiet rest; they liked their tranquil and ordered nature.

On 21 May 1917 a Royal Charter established the Imperial War Graves Commission, more formally to confirm the principles which Ware and his colleagues had already enunciated. Regulations stressed that the headstones should be uniform, with no distinction made on account of rank.

The stones have never varied. They are 2 ft 8 in in height and 1 ft 3 in wide, with the top gently curved at the ends. Variations exist, however, in the case of foreign nationals or civilians. Each stone bears the badge of the service, corps or national emblem, together with the name, rank and number of the serviceman and his decorations. The relevant religious emblem is included unless the serviceman had given no religion on his enlistment papers or described himself as 'Atheist', as some did. The epitaph inscription was chosen by relatives, generally next of kin. Headstones of servicemen awarded the Victoria Cross bear an outsize emblem of the decoration in place of any other cross.

The headstones of winners of the Victoria Cross are engraved with the cross itself. This is the burial place of Captain Clarence Jeffries. Behind his headstone is one of the German blockhouses in Tyne Cot Cemetery, Passchendaele.

Sometimes there is doubt about the precise location of a soldier's burial in a cemetery. In this case 'Believed to be buried in this cemetery' appears on the face of the stone, at the top. Many graves were destroyed in later battles, especially in 1918, so 'Known to be buried in this cemetery' or 'Buried near this spot' are engraved on the stones. Where a man's name appears on a stone his remains are definitely under that stone. Where a man's identity is unknown the stone bears the words 'A soldier of the Great War' or 'An officer of the Great War – a

Scottish regiment' or any information that might give some indication of the unknown soldier's nationality, rank and unit. I have seen 'A Scottish soldier, a Highland regiment'. Obviously the soldier's remains, when found, still had a kilt or sporran in place but in such poor condition that the tartan could not be discerned.

Graves of those servicemen completely unidentified bear the inscription 'Known unto God', a phrase suggested by Rudyard Kipling, who had lost his son in the war. Lieutenant John Kipling had no known grave until 1993, when clever

Ors Communal Cemetery, near Sambre Canal. The poet Wilfred Owen's grave is among those here.

202

analysis suggested that an officer buried in a particular grave was probably that of the young Kipling.

Rudyard Kipling also suggested the wording on the Stone of Remembrance, found in all but the very small cemeteries. It is 'Their Name Liveth for Evermore' (Ecclesiasticus 44:14). The Stone of Remembrance – often called 'The War Stone' – was designed by Sir Edwin Lutyens. The Cross of Sacrifice, part of all the cemeteries, was designed by Sir Reginald Blomfield.

The English-type gardens, so admired by all visitors to the cemeteries, were designed by Gertrude Jekyll. Work began

immediately after the war ended but it was easier to deal with those burial grounds which had been designated permanent cemeteries. The first gardens were complete, 'with all flowers blooming', in 1920 and they included two in the fighting areas, at Forceville and Louvencourt.

By now battlefield pilgrimages had commenced and the IWGC worked closely with the British Legion and Thomas Cook. While the commission was never a tour arranger, it has given help and advice to millions of pilgrims.

With such large numbers of 'missing' in the official records it was imperative to

The Menin Gate, and beyond it the tower of the Cloth Hall. Unveiled in 1927, the great gate is a memorial to the missing of the Ypres Salient.

begin work on memorials to them. Appropriate sites were selected, the land was obtained from the French and Belgian governments, and in the 1920s the work began. The largest were the huge Thiepval Arch, towering over so much of the Somme department, and the Menin Gate, Ypres. Each of the dominions built its own memorials to the missing. Nearly every memorial had graves around it or close to it.

The commission's network of care is all-embracing. For instance, by contract it cares for private service memorials and some individual graves of soldiers buried before the IWGC came into being.

Most cemeteries have a recess in a wall, generally close to the entrance, where a bronze door protects a copy of the cemetery or memorial register as well as a visitors' book. Sadly, there are some significant but smaller cemeteries where these books are not provided. Toronto Avenue Cemetery, in Ploegsteert Wood, is an example. It is important to Australians, since all the seventy-eight men buried here are AIF soldiers.

A cemetery register has a simple sketch map showing the location of other cemeteries in the district and a plan of the cemetery's layout. Each cemetery is divided into plots and rows and each headstone has a number carved into its shoulder. In the register the number of a plot is indicated by a Roman numeral, the row by a capital letter and the grave by a number. For example, in Adelaide Cemetery, Villers Bretonneux, the grave

The 1st Australian Tunnelling Company memorial at Hill 60, Ypres. Under appalling conditions, these military miners burrowed under enemy positions to place vast quantities of explosives.

of Sergeant David Allen MM, 32nd Battalion, AIF, is III.E.8.

Even in a large cemetery any grave can be located in a few minutes. Occasionally, the CWGC departs from this system and uses Arabic numerals for the plot number. Some cemeteries are too small for the graves to be set out in plots, hence the graves appear in the register without Roman numerals.

The CWGC cemeteries are full of interest. Study of a soldier's army number, his date of death and the name of his unit can often indicate the battle or offensive in which he died. A cemetery that has many 'unknowns', as in the case of Tyne Cot Cemetery, is obviously a battlefield cemetery. Where a cemetery is large but every burial is identified by name it can be inferred that the soldiers buried there died of wounds in nearby hospitals and were buried directly from the hospitals. Lijssenthoek, Poperinge, is such a cemetery. Introductory notes in the cemetery register often give information about the actions which led to the burial in a particular cemetery.

Some headstones show two regimental or army badges conjoined in the engraving, for instance the New Zealand fernleaf emblem conjoined with the Australian rising sun emblem. This indicates that the remains of the soldiers have been buried together because they could not be separated for identification. A cemetery with many such shared headstones is Bailleul Communal Cemetery Extension.

Anzac brothers-in-arms in Bailleul Communal Cemetery Extension, northern France. The conjoined badges indicate that the remains of the two men, killed during the Battle of Messines, could not be separated.

In most cemeteries the stones are set at even distances apart, indicating quite separate burials. In other burial grounds rows of headstones are set firmly against one another, in shoulder-to-shoulder style. The soldiers beneath them have been the subject of a trench burial. This might have been done for the sake of speed, if the men concerned all died on the same day. The burial ground could have been under fire at the time of the interments. An interesting example is Rue Petillon Cemetery, in the Fleurbaix area south of Armentières. In the Battle of Fromelles of 12–20 July 1916, 5,333 Australians became casualties in 19 hours. Those men whose remains could quickly be retrieved or who died of wounds after evacuation from the battlefield were buried promptly because Rue Petillon was itself a dangerous place to be.

Many frequent battlefield visitors have come to understand the lore of military cemeteries and in their research they learn much about some of the soldiers.

They regard it as a form of remembrance.

By 1960 there were grumblings about the word 'Imperial' in the title of the organization. For some people this was too 'colonial' a word, with connotations of British chauvinism. In March that year the title was changed to Commonwealth War Graves Commission. It was an expensive change because the thousands of cemetery nameplates and direction signs had to be replaced.

The CWGC is represented in all regions where British Commonwealth servicemen and women are buried. The main offices are:

Main CWGC office: 2 Marlow Road
Maidenhead
Berkshire SL6 7DX
United Kingdom

Tel: (0628) 834221

France: Rue Angèle Richard
Beaurains
62012 Arras Cedex

Tel: (21) 230324

Belgium: Elverdingestraat 82
B–8900 Ieper
(Ypres)

Tel: (057) 200118

The cost of the commission's work is shared by the governments of the United Kingdom, Canada, Australia, South Africa, New Zealand and India (Pakistan opted out in 1990), in proportion to the numbers of their graves.

Many international agreements support and protect the CWGC's work in various countries. Many governments bought land at state expense and then presented it in perpetuity to the commission, whose work is governed by Royal Charter.

Information about individual burials or commemorations, about cemeteries and other matters relating to servicemen who were killed or who are listed as missing is available in all the former British Empire countries through their respective Department of Veterans Affairs.

In Australia the Office of Australian War Graves is PO Box 21, Woden A.C.T. 2602. In New Zealand, the Department of Internal Affairs is the relevant agency for the CWGC. The address is The Secretary, Department of Internal Affairs, Private Bag, Wellington, New Zealand. For Canada, the address is Secretary-General, Canadian Agency, CWGC, 284 Wellington St, Ottawa, Ontario KIA OP4, Canada. For South Africa, Secretary, South African Agency, PO Box 1554, Pretoria 0001, South Africa.

AN EXCEPTION TO THE RULE

To every statement made about the Western Front there is an exception and this applies in an interesting way to headstones in Commonwealth War Graves Commission cemeteries. As stated earlier, stones have precise dimensions and style and no exceptions were to be permitted, but exceptions there are. In a few cases a soldier has his regulation headstone together with, right alongside, a grave marker erected by his family. I know of two like this in Heilly Station Cemetery and one in Qerrieu Cemetery, both in the Somme river valley. All three non-regulation markers are short columns mounted on marble blocks. One headstone at Locre, near Bailleul, is just outside the cemetery because the family of the dead officer, a member of the Redmond family, who were staunch nationalists, did not want him to lie amid hated Englishmen. This was a pity because he had served with Englishmen, but at least his headstone is the familiar CWGC stone.

The remarkable exception to the rule is the gravestone of Second Lieutenant Herbert Crowle of the Tenth Battalion, AIF, who died of wounds in a field hospital at Puchevillers, north-east of Amiens.

Following Bert's death, his widow and brother quickly arranged for a French mason to erect a stone of their own design. Being wider and higher than the

The privately erected grave marker of Driver J.F. Farrell in Qerrieu Cemetery, between Albert and Amiens. He also has a regulation military headstone.

other stones, as well as different in shape and slightly different in colour, the Crowle stone stands out from the rows of standard markers. The authorities decided to allow it to remain, and had they been aware of the letter that Bert wrote from his deathbed they would have been certain that their decision was correct.

On 24 August 1916 Bert Crowle wrote to his wife Beatrice:

Dearest Beat and Bill,

Just a line you must be prepared for the worst to happen any day. It is no use trying to hide things. I am in terrible agony. Had I been brought in at once I had a hope. But now gas gangrene has set in and it is so bad that the doctor could not save it [his leg] by taking it off as it had gone too far and the only hope is that the salts they have put on may drain the gangrene out otherwise there is no hope. The pain is much worse today so the doctor gave me some morphia, which has eased me a little but still is awful. Tomorrow I shall know the worst as the dressing was to be left on for 3 days and tomorrow is the third day it smells rotten. I was hit running out to see the other officer who was with me but badly wounded. I ran too far as I was in a hurry and he had passed the word down to return, it kept coming down and there was nothing to do but go up and see what he meant, I got two machine-gun bullets in the thigh another glanced off by my water bottle and another by the periscope I had in my pocket, you will see that they will send my things home. It was during the operations around Mouquet Farm, about 20 days I was in the thick of the attack on Pozières as I had just about done my duty. Even if I get over it I will never go back to the war as they have taken pounds of flesh out of my buttock, my word they look after us well here. I am in the officers ward and can get anything I want to eat or drink but I just drink all day changing the drinks as I take a fancy. The Stretcher Bearers could not get the wounded out any way than over the top and across the open. They had to carry me four miles with a man waving a red cross flag in front and the

Lt. Bert Crowle's unique grave marker in Puchevillers military cemetery, France. Crowle, an Australian, died of wounds in a nearby hospital. All other British and Empire headstones are the type seen

Germans did not open fire on us. Well dearest I have had a rest, the pain is getting worse and worse. I am very sorry dear, but still you will be well provided for I am easy on that score. So cheer up dear I could write on a lot but I am nearly unconscious. Give my love to dear Bill and yourself, do take care of yourself and him.

Your loving husband
Bert.

CHAPTER ELEVEN

PLACES TO STAY, TOURIST OFFICES, TOUR OPERATORS

Battlefield pilgrims and students of the First World War have long known that the Western Front in France and Belgium is an absorbingly interesting place, but now many 'ordinary' tourists are discovering it. It offers not only battlefields, memorials, museums and the beautiful and intriguing military cemeteries but lovely countryside and attractive towns, many of them ancient.

To cater for the increasing number of visitors many hotels and guesthouses have opened, while there are more and better caravanning and camping grounds. For touring purposes France can be divided into battlefield regions.

SOMME

This is a region of compelling interest for people from Britain and the countries of the old empire. While the entire department is entrancing, for battlefield visits certain towns are more important than others.

ALBERT

There is no more central and convenient base than Albert. I recommend the Hôtel de la Paix, 45 rue Victor Hugo, 80300 Albert; Hôtel de la Basilique, 4 rue Gambette, Albert 80300; and Le Relais Fleurie, 56 avenue Faidherbe, 80300 Albert.

AMIENS

A city rather than a town, Amiens is a historic place with a variety of hotels from one-star to five-star, but down the scale some hotels have no restaurant. Several hotel chains are represented – Fimotel, Ibis, Open Hotel, Vidéotel, Campanile and Formula (one-star). One of the cheapest is Central Anzac, 17 rue Alexandre Patton, Amiens 80000. A

An artist's impression of the Victory March in the Champs d'Elysées, Paris, 1918.

good two-star is Hôtel Ibis Le Centrum, rue du Mal-de Lattre de Tassigny, Amiens 80000.

ASSEVILLERS

On the Autoroute du Nord, linking Calais to Paris, Assevillers is a motorway stop, together with a three-star Mercure Hôtel. It is another base for Somme visits and further afield.

PERONNE

One of the best bases for visits to places connected with the second Battle of the Somme, the events of 8 August 1918 and the upper Aisne, right through to the Hindenburg Line north of St Quentin. I recommend the Hostellerie des Ramparts, 21 rue Beaubois, Peronne, 80200 and Hôtel St Claude, 42 place Louis Daudre, Peronne 80200. Peronne has become even more important for visitors to the battlefields since L'Historial de la Grand Guerre was opened in 1992. It is the official museum of the First World War, housed in a purpose-built structure within the town's ancient castle. It is an imaginative and well-organized museum.

PAS DE CALAIS

Arras has so much to offer that visitors need to stay for the city itself, but it is also the best base for visiting Vimy Ridge and its several places of interest. It is also a convenient base for Neuve Chapelle, Le Cateau, Cambrai and Bullecourt. Arras has many hotels. I recommend the three-star Mercure Hôtel and the Hôtel Moderne in Boulevarde Faidherbe. The railway station square is a convenient place for meals and the station itself has an excellent restaurant.

CAMBRAI

Useful as a base for the battlefields of 1914 and 1918, Cambrai is a most attractive city with several hotels, as well as restaurants and cafés galore. I recommend the three-star Château de la Motte Fenelon in Allée St Roch and the two-star Campanile, Route de la Bassee.

VERDUN–REIMS

REIMS

A dignified and historic city, Reims is one of the best bases for touring the Meuse and Argonne battlefields, together with Verdun and St Mihiel. The numerous hotels include Novotel Reims and Mercure Reims, both three-star establishments.

VERDUN

Three days are necessary to visit Verdun properly but much can be seen in one long summer day. The best hotel is only a three-star, Coq Hardi at 8 avenue de la Victoire, while the best in the cheaper bracket is the Bellevue, 1 rondpoint du Maréchal de Lattre de Tassigny.

LILLE

I prefer to visit the Ypres Salient from Ypres itself but some experienced Western Front visitors like to operate from Lille. Lille is certainly a good base for French Flanders and further east, even as far as Mons. Lille Lomme Novotel is a handy hotel but the Mercure at Lille Centre is more convenient for getting about this large and busy city.

BELGIUM AND FRENCH FLANDERS

YPRES

This historic jewel of a small city has so much to offer that a hotel in the Grote Markt is necessary for visitors who want to walk about the city. Here are the Regina and Old Tom, and a short distance away along Boterstraat is the Hostellerie St Nicholas. A few blocks distant, near the railway station, is the Continental. The Ariane is also not far from the Grote Markt but many tour parties stay at the Rabbit, a mile from the Menin Gate. No part of the salient is further than 8 miles from Ypres.

POPERINGE

This interesting small town, only 7 miles west of Ypres, has at least four places where battlefield visitors might stay. They are: Amfora Hotel in the Grote Markt, 8970 Poperinge; Belfort Hotel, also in the Grote Markt; Palace Hotel, Ieperstraat; and Talbot House, Gasthuisstraat. Talbot House is the building where Padre Tubby Clayton founded Toc H. Soldiers on short leave used Talbot House as a place for rest, recreation and sleep, and their benign presence can still be felt there. Rooms are available to all visitors, not merely to Toc H members, and while no meals are provided, guests may prepare their own meals in the kitchen.

ARMENTIÈRES

For people influenced by 'Mademoiselle from Armentières' the large town of this name is a good base for exploring all of Belgian and French Flanders. I recommend the Hôtel Joly at 12 rue du Président Kennedy and the Hôtel-Restaurant Au Prophete, Place de la Gare. There are two other cheaper hotels with no restaurant service. They are Hôtel Albert, 26 rue R. Shuman and Hôtel des Arcades, 7 rue de la Gare.

While I have listed hotels here I prefer to stay, especially in France, at Chambres d'Hôtes establishments. In effect these are small and reasonably priced private hotels. The following establishments are recommended:

BAVELINCOURT

Madame Noel Valengin, Bavelincourt, 80260 Villers Bocage. In this hamlet, 10 miles west of Albert, is an old chateau in which soldiers were billeted. It is now a guesthouse with five bedrooms, one of them en suite.

POZIÈRES

Café des Routiers, 80300 France. This travellers' guesthouse and restaurant has eight bedrooms. It is in the middle of the Somme battlefield and was itself built on the rubble of the Pozières killing field.

GINCHY

M. and Mme Roger Salmain run a Chambre d'Hôte in rue de Flers, a centre of battle in 1916.

GRANDCOURT

M. and Mme Louis Bellengez's Chambres d'Hote is virtually on the 1916 front line and is part of their farmhouse. About 7 miles from Albert, it is a good base for visiting the left flank of the British 1 July 1916 offensive.

MAIN TOURIST OFFICES ON THE WESTERN FRONT

Somme Region Tourist Office: 21 rue Ernest Cauvin, 80000 Amiens, France. Tel: (22) 922639. Fax: (22) 927747.

Ypres Tourist Office: Stadhuis, Grote Markt, B–8900, Ieper, Belgium.

Calais Region Tourist Office: 44 Grande Rue, 62200 Boulogne-sur-Mer, France.

North Region Tourist Department: 15–17 rue du Nouveau Siècle, 59800 Lille, France.

Albert Tourist Office: 9 rue Gambetta, Albert 80300, France.

Peronne Tourist Office: Place du Château, Peronne 80200, France.

Poperinge Tourist Office: Town Hall, Grote Markt, Poperinge, Belgium.

WESTERN FRONT TOUR OPERATORS

Flanders Tours, 4 Spencer House, 45a Crystal Palace Road, London SE22 9EX. Official tour operator for the Western Front Association.

Major and Mrs Holt's Tours, 15 Market Street, Sandwich, Kent.

Martin Middlebrook, 48 Linden Way, Boston, Lincolnshire OE21 9DS.

No-Man's-Land Tours, 155 Bedfont Close, Bedfont, Feltham, Middlesex TW14 8LQ.

Roberts' Battlefield Tours, 7 Titan House, Calleva Park, Aldermaston, Berkshire RG7 4QW.

Goodwin European Battlefield Tours (History Club), 194 Dominic Drive, London SE9 3LE.

BIBLIOGRAPHY

There is little point in listing books which, however admirable, are out of print. The following titles are not only desirable but obtainable.

Coombs, Rose M., *Before Endeavours Fade*, Battle of Britain Prints International Ltd, London, 1977, and other editions. This is the essential on-the-spot guidebook.

Ellis, John, *Eye-Deep in Hell: Life in the Trenches 1914–18*, Fontana, London, 1977.

Gilbert, Martin, *First World War Atlas*, Weidenfeld and Nicolson, London, 1970.

Gliddon, Gerald, *When the Barrage Lifts*, a topographical history and commentary on the Battle of the Somme 1916, Gliddon Books, Norfolk, 1987. Reprinted 1994, Alan Sutton Publishing Ltd.

Haythornthwaite, Philip J. *The World War One Source Book*, Arms and Armour Press, London, 1992.

Herwig, Holger L. and Heyman, Neil M., *Biographical Dictionary of World War I*, Greenwood Press, Connecticut, 1982.

Holt, Tonie and Valmai, *Battlefields of the First World War*, Pavilion Books Ltd, London, 1993.

Laffin, John, *Guide to Australian Battlefields of the Western Front*, Kangaroo Press, Sydney, 1992. On sale in Britain.

Laffin, John, *The Western Front Illustrated*, Alan Sutton Publishing, Gloucestershire, 1992.

Laffin, John, *Panorama of the Western Front*, Alan Sutton Publishing, Gloucestershire, 1993.

Shores, C., Franks, N. and Guest, R., *Above the Trenches: A Complete Record of the Fighter Aces and Units of the British Empire Air Forces 1915–1920*, Grub Street, London, 1990.

INDEX

Illustration references are in *italics* after text references.